books**online**

Read this book online today:

With SAP PRESS BooksOnline we offer you online access to knowledge from the leading SAP experts. Whether you use it as a beneficial supplement or as an alternative to the printed book, with SAP PRESS BooksOnline you can:

- Access your book anywhere, at any time. All you need is an Internet connection.
- Perform full text searches on your book and on the entire SAP PRESS library.
- Build your own personalized SAP library.

The SAP PRESS customer advantage:

Register this book today at *www.sap-press.com* and obtain exclusive free trial access to its online version. If you like it (and we think you will), you can choose to purchase permanent, unrestricted access to the online edition at a very special price!

Here's how to get started:

1. Visit *www.sap-press.com*.
2. Click on the link for SAP PRESS BooksOnline and login (or create an account).
3. Enter your free trial license key, shown below in the corner of the page.
4. Try out your online book with full, unrestricted access for a limited time!

Your personal free trial **license key**
for this online book is:

kys4-xbt8-5gje-cvhp

100 Things You Should Know About
ABAP® Workbench

 **PRESS**

SAP PRESS is a joint initiative of SAP and Galileo Press. The know-how offered by SAP specialists combined with the expertise of the Galileo Press publishing house offers the reader expert books in the field. SAP PRESS features first-hand information and expert advice, and provides useful skills for professional decision-making.

SAP PRESS offers a variety of books on technical and business related topics for the SAP user. For further information, please visit our website: *www.sap-press.com*.

James Wood and Shaan Parvaze
Web Dynpro ABAP—The Comprehensive Guide
2013, app. 850 pp., hardcover
ISBN 978-1-59229-416-9

Tanmaya Gupta
ABAP Data Dictionary
2011, 403 pp., hardcover
ISBN 978-1-59229-379-7

James Wood
ABAP Cookbook—Programming Recipes for Everyday Solutions
2010, 548 pp., hardcover
ISBN 978-1-59229-326-1

Horst Keller and Sascha Krüger
ABAP Objects—ABAP Programming in SAP NetWeaver (2nd Edition)
2007, 1059 pp., hardcover
ISBN 978-1-59229-079-6

Abdulbasıt Gülşen

100 Things You Should Know About
ABAP® Workbench

Galileo Press

Bonn • Boston

Galileo Press is named after the Italian physicist, mathematician and philosopher Galileo Galilei (1564–1642). He is known as one of the founders of modern science and an advocate of our contemporary, heliocentric worldview. His words *Eppur si muove* (And yet it moves) have become legendary. The Galileo Press logo depicts Jupiter orbited by the four Galilean moons, which were discovered by Galileo in 1610.

Editor Laura Korslund
Acquisitions Editor Kelly Grace Harris
Copyeditor Julie McNamee
Cover Design Graham Geary
Layout Design Graham Geary
Production Graham Geary
Typesetting Publishers' Design and Production Services, Inc.
Printed and bound in the United States of America, on paper from sustainable sources

ISBN 978-1-59229-427-5

© 2012 by Galileo Press Inc., Boston (MA)
1st edition 2012

Library of Congress Cataloging-in-Publication Data
Gülşen, Abdulbasıt
100 things you should know about ABAP Workbench / Abdulbasıt Gülşen.
— 1st edition.
pages ; cm
ISBN 978-1-59229-427-5 — ISBN 1-59229-427-8 1. ABAP/4 (Computer program
language) 2. Enterprise resource planning. 3. Application
software—Development. I. Title. II. Title: One hundred things you should
know about ABAP Workbench.
QA76.73.A12G85 2013
005.13'3—dc23
2012020675

Contents at a Glance

Dear Reader,

Here at SAP PRESS, we work with authors from all over the world. In this day and age, you might think that editor/author communication should be fairly seamless what with cell phones, email, and other forms of instant communication. However, this is often *not* the case—our authors are very busy people! However, I was very lucky when I became Abdulbasıt Gülşen's editor—even though he was very busy trying to balance his job and write this book, he was always quick to respond, and amazing at meeting his deadlines (thank you!). And despite the fact that there are seven pretty important hours separating Turkey and Massachusetts, Abdulbasıt replied to any question or email so quickly, it was almost like working in the same office and in the same time zone!

With all of my excitement for stellar communication skills aside, I'm thrilled to present the latest *100 Things* book to you. Abdulbasıt constantly impressed me with the amount of time he spent selecting the best and most useful tips for you in your work with the ABAP Workbench—in fact, he even discarded a few of the original tips in favor of writing new and better ones. I'm confident that you'll find it just as rewarding to navigate this book as I did, and better yet, you'll find that helpful hint that will help you on your way towards becoming a master ABAP developer, no matter what your experience is!

We at SAP PRESS are always eager to hear your opinion. What do you think about *100 Things You Should Know About the ABAP Workbench*? As your comments and suggestions are our most useful tools to help us make our books the best they can be, we encourage you to visit our website at *www.sap-press.com* and share your feedback.

Thank you for purchasing a book from SAP PRESS!

Laura Korslund
Editor, SAP PRESS

Galileo Press
Boston, MA

laura.korslund@galileo-press.com
www.sap-press.com

Contents

Acknowledgments

This book has been written in roughly 6 months, but the tips were gathered from the past 12 years of my SAP career. Every single person I worked with or who helped me to learn even a single line of code directly or indirectly during this period of time has contributions in the book. I would like to thank all of them for their support to my success.

As this is my first book project, I didn't know much about the tough steps of writing a book. It is more challenging than it is seen from the outside world. The SAP PRESS team, Kelly Harris and Laura Korslund, made great efforts at each step of this process to help me finish the book. I would like to thank them and the production team for their great support in helping to bring out the book at the highest quality standards.

I would like to add a special thanks to my family: my mother for giving me life and also always making me feel her love around me, my father for teaching me to work hard and overcome difficulties, and my siblings for always being with me in the good and bad times. I also express my thanks to my mother-in-law who motivated me a lot to complete this book and father-in law who shared his own experiences on writing a book.

Finally, I want to give all my love and gratitude to my wife Görkem Anıl Gülşen, who always walked together with me for many years and encouraged me to write this book. This book wouldn't be possible without her support. Writing a book takes a lot of sacrifice, including many days of work that take time from your life. She didn't allow me to spend this time away from her; instead, she always stayed with me and became part of the book with her patience, support, and understanding.

Introduction

SAP is continuously adding new products and solutions into the product portfolio to keep the platform up to date and meet the latest technology trends. Although some of these new products need to be developed in different programming languages, ABAP® still stands as a major programming language for software development in the SAP platform. It is a simple but powerful language for developers to build enterprise applications.

Several tools are available in the ABAP Workbench that make the development process easy and efficient. In this book, you'll find 100 little-known tips and tricks that teach you quick and practical techniques to solve your problems and increase your productivity while using the ABAP Workbench tools. This book neither gives detailed tutorials explaining how to use these ABAP Workbench tools nor teaches the ABAP programming language. Each tip has only 3-5 pages that focus on the specific problem or topic that you can immediately use in your daily work. If you want to get more background detail about any tool explained in the book, we recommend searching the SAP PRESS catalog for another book focused on the tool or refer to the SAP Community Network (*http://scn.sap.com*) or official documentation provided by SAP (*http://help.sap.com*).

The ABAP Workbench has many tools and features that cannot be limited to 100 tips. Tips that are included in the book are selected from the wide range of topics mostly to give you workarounds to perform your daily tasks in a more efficient way. Some tips in the book require expert-level knowledge, and some can be very simple for ABAP experts, but generally they are selected to address both beginner and advanced ABAP programmers. You can put this book into your library and consult it when you want to read tips about specific tools, or you can read from start to end. I was excited to learn many of these tips, and I hope you'll feel the same when you read tips that will save you time and effort on a daily basis.

Tips in the book are divided into nine different parts. In the first four parts, you'll find tips that mostly help you to improve your ABAP development capabilities by providing practical, alternative workaround solutions while you're using the ABAP Workbench tools to develop an ABAP program, such as the ABAP Editor, the Function Builder, and the Class Builder.

In Part 5, we move into the analysis phase of ABAP programming. In this part, you'll find very useful tips on the ABAP Debugger to help you find bugs in your ABAP programs. You'll see how the new ABAP Debugger is improved after it's launched. You'll also notice the latest improvements of the ABAP Debugger in SAP NetWeaver 7.3. We've added a footnote about the version restrictions in the individual tip title in all that apply.

You might also see some differences in the step-by-step procedures or screenshots because of the version difference. We've used the SAP NetWeaver 7.3 system to describe the step-by-step procedures and provide the screenshots. If you're using a different version, please note that there may be small differences on the tools.

Part 6 is also focused on problem analysis in ABAP programs. You'll find tips for various analysis tools in the ABAP Workbench. You'll learn practical ways of improving the code quality and find performance bottlenecks arising from wrong database or memory usages. There are also useful tips that will help you to analyze SAP Business Workflow problems.

In Part 7, you'll learn practical ways of using the ABAP Data Dictionary tools. The ABAP Data Dictionary has very broad features that can't be limited to a small part in a book. This part lists the most useful and practical tips on using the ABAP Data Dictionary tools.

Enhancement tips listed in Part 8 are included to give you practical ways of using the Enhancement Framework, which is also one of the most useful parts of the ABAP Workbench. In this part, you'll see different usages of the Enhancement Framework that will save a lot of time during patches or system upgrades.

Finally, in Part 9, you'll see some tips on Web Dynpro ABAP. Of course, it's impossible to fit tips about Web Dynpro ABAP in a small part of this book. We've added some tips about Web Dynpro ABAP that are mostly related to the other ABAP Workbench tools. If you want more details, we highly recommend the books *Getting Started with Web Dynpro ABAP* (SAP PRESS, 2010) and *Web Dynpro ABAP—The Comprehensive Guide* (SAP PRESS, 2013).

Part 1

Object Navigator

Things You'll Learn in this Section

The Object Navigator is the central point in the ABAP Workbench that developers use to create and modify development objects, which can then be accessed with Transaction SE80. It provides you with a hierarchical display of all development objects, allowing you to easily display and maintain objects using the relevant development tools. Objects are separated into groups (such as PROGRAM, PACKAGE, FUNCTION GROUP, etc.), and for each group, you can select individual objects to see the list of subobjects contained in the main object. You can also double-click any object on the list to open the relevant development tool without having to remember the specific transaction code or menu path.

Because the Object Navigator is the main development tool for ABAP developers, it's critical to use this tool efficiently. In this part of the book, we provide tips and tricks to increase the productivity of developers while using the Object Navigator.

Tip 1

Building Package Hierarchies to Organize Development Objects

You can better manage your development objects by creating package hierarchies.

The *packaging* concept is widely used in software development to modularize and encapsulate development objects. The Package Builder tool in ABAP Workbench is used for this purpose. It allows developers to organize development objects in separate packages in terms of functionality, usage, and the category they should belong to. Development objects are usually put into large packages grouped by functional modules (ZMM, ZFI, ZHCM, etc.). However, in big development projects, splitting development objects into separate packages isn't enough. In this tip, we'll show you a better way to organize these objects to make them easier to manage by building your own package hierarchy.

And Here's How ...

Three types of packages are used to build a package hierarchy: *structure package*, *main package*, and *development package*. A structure package is created to contain all packages at the top level. For example, you can separate the development objects for a single module or project into different packages according to their technical or business attributes, but then combine them into a single top-level structure package to be able to access the development objects easily. Then, main packages need to be created and added into the structure package. Finally, development packages are created to store development objects. The following rules must be satisfied when creating package hierarchies:

▶ The root package in a package hierarchy must always be a structure package.

▶ Structure and main packages can't contain development objects.

▶ A main package can be a subpackage of a structure or main package.

▶ A development package can be a subpackage of a main or development package.

Main and development packages can be nested to any level to create the desired hierarchy as shown in Figure 1.

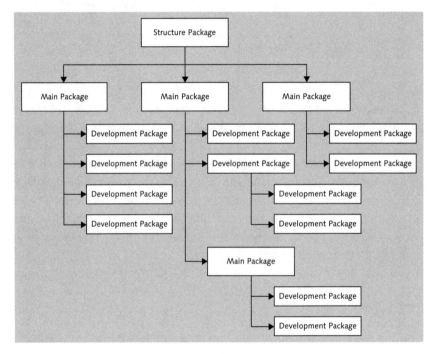

⌃ *Figure 1* *Package Hierarchy Showing All Possible Package Assignments*

Now let's start to build a package hierarchy. We have to create the structure, main, and development packages.

Create a Structure Package

To create a structure package, follow these steps:

1. Go to Transaction SE21 to open Package Builder (alternatively, you can use the Repository Browser with Transaction SE80).

2. Enter the name of the package you're creating and click CREATE.

3. Enter the package attributes (see Figure 2).

4. In the PACKAGE LEVEL field, select S STRUCTURE PACKAGE.

5. Save.

Package Builder: Create Package	✕
Name	Z100THINGS
Description	100 Things You Should Know about ABAP Workbench
Application Component	CA
Software Component	HOME
Transport Layer	
Superpackage	
Package Level	S Structure Package ▾

⌃ *Figure 2* Create Package Dialog

Create a Main Package

To create a main package, follow these steps:

1. Repeat the same procedure as for the structure package.

2. In the SUPERPACKAGE field, select any of the previously created structure or main packages

3. In the PACKAGE LEVEL field, select MAIN PACKAGE.

4. Save.

Create all main packages using the same procedure, and assign superpackages accordingly.

Create a Development Package

To create a development package, follow these steps:

1. Repeat the same procedure as for the structure package.

2. In the SUPERPACKAGE field, select any of the previously created main or development packages.

3. In the PACKAGE LEVEL field, select DEVELOPMENT PACKAGE.

4. Save.

Create all development packages using the same procedure, and assign superpackages accordingly.

You have now created all of the necessary packages and built a package hierarchy. Next, go to Transaction SE80 and open the structure package that you have created as the root package. You can see all embedded main and development packages in a hierarchical object list under the structure package. In Figure 3, you can see a package view showing the sample nested hierarchy.

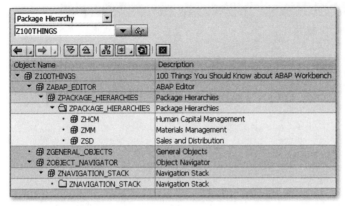

⌃ *Figure 3 Package View Showing the Nested Hierarchy*

Double-click on any of the packages in the hierarchy to see the details of the package. Subpackages of a package are shown in the SUBPACKAGES tab in the package details screen (see Figure 4). You can create or delete a package or move another package below the current package from this screen.

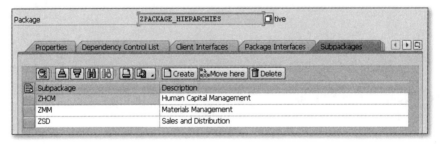

⌃ *Figure 4 Subpackage List*

Note that although you technically can move a package to below another package, it isn't fully supported as of SAP NetWeaver release 7.3. Use this feature at your own discretion.

Tip 2

Using the Reuse Library to Find Reusable Software Objects, Documentation, and Examples

You can use the Reuse Library to access examples, documentation, and reusable software objects to improve your ABAP experience.

Typically, when you're learning a new programming language, you start by learning the syntax and developing your first *Hello World* application. This is the easiest part of the never-ending story. No matter how much experience you have, you'll always need to find help documents, sample programs, and reusable software components. At that point, the ABAP Workbench offers the *Reuse Library* to help you speed up your development processes or improve your ABAP experience. In this tip, we'll help you get familiar with this tool.

✓ And Here's How ...

The Reuse Library is a tool that helps you find reusable software products. You can access it with Transaction SE83 or by selecting ENVIRONMENT • REUSE LIBRARY in the Object Navigator.

On the left side of the screen, you'll see a hierarchical list of reuse products. You can display the reuse product on the right side by double-clicking on its name. Figure 1 shows an example of a reuse product.

⌃ *Figure 1* Reuse Product

The reuse product information is categorized on the following tabs:

▶ OVERVIEW
Contains basic information about the reuse product.

▶ DOCUMENTATION
Contains help documents about the reuse product and gives you detailed information before using it in your programs.

▶ EXAMPLES
Contains sample applications that give you an idea about the reuse product. You can directly start the application or navigate to the source code from the Reuse Library. You can also add sample applications into your worklist with the ADD TO WORKLIST button on the toolbar.

▶ PROGRAM OBJECTS
Provides easy access to program objects that allow you to reuse the product. You can add the program objects into your worklist with the same procedure as in the EXAMPLES tab.

▶ DEVELOPMENT SUPPORT
Provides tools such as wizards, generators, or templates to speed up the use of the reuse product.

The Reuse Library includes the following popular topics:

▶ ALV GRID CONTROL

▶ HTML VIEWER

▸ TEXT EDIT

▸ TREE CONTROLS

Creating a Reuse Product

You can also modify or create your own reuse products and libraries. Follow these steps to create a reuse product:

1. Go to Transaction SLIBP.

2. Enter the name of the reuse product and click CREATE.

3. Enter the description into the PRODUCT NAME field and click SAVE.

4. Select the package and save.

5. Maintain the information on the GENERAL DATA, OVERVIEW, DOCUMENTATION, EXAMPLES, PROGRAM OBJECTS, and DEVELOPMENT SUPPORT tabs, and then save.

Creating a Reuse Library

Follow these steps to create your own Reuse Library:

1. Go to Transaction SLIBN.

2. Enter the name of the Reuse Library and click CREATE.

3. Enter the description and select the visibility:

    ▸ PUBLIC: The reuse library is visible to everyone in Transaction SE83.

    ▸ PRIVATE: A parameter transaction needs to be created to display this type of library.

4. Select the package and SAVE.

5. Use the SUBNODES and SAME LEVEL buttons to create tree nodes and insert reuse products, and then save.

You can subscribe to public libraries with the LIBRARIES button on the toolbar in Transaction SE83. A list of the available libraries opens, and you can subscribe to any of them by selecting and moving to the SUBSCRIBED LIBRARIES list as shown in Figure 2.

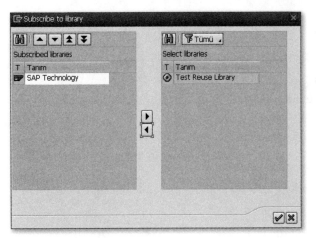

≪ Figure 2 Subscribe to a Library

When you subscribe to a library, it becomes available in the Reuse Library.

On the other hand, you must create a *parameter transaction* to access private libraries. This feature allows you to assign Reuse Libraries to different user groups. Follow this procedure:

1. Go to Transaction SE93.

2. Enter the TRANSACTION CODE, and click CREATE.

3. Enter the SHORT TEXT.

4. Select TRANSACTION WITH PARAMETERS from the list, and click CONTINUE.

5. Enter "SE83_START" in the TRANSACTION field, and select the SKIP INITIAL SCREEN checkbox.

6. Fill in the DEFAULT VALUES table as shown in Figure 3. You can combine up to nine Reuse Libraries by specifying their names in the DEFAULT VALUES table.

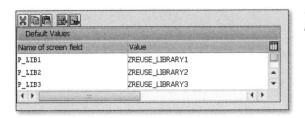

≪ Figure 3 Combining Reuse Libraries in a Parameter Transaction

Tip 3

Accessing Your Previous Navigation Steps with the Navigation Stack

You can easily return to previous navigation steps with the Navigation Stack tool, which helps you make use of drill-down type navigation capabilities of the Object Navigator.

While working on a development object in the Object Navigator, you might want to jump to another object to make a little change and then return to the first object. However, sometimes it can be difficult to remember all of the steps you took and return to them easily. To assist you, the Navigation Stack tool keeps a list of these steps and allows you to easily navigate back and forth in the list.

✓ And Here's How ...

The Object Navigator allows you the following navigation options while you're using different ABAP Workbench development tools:

▸ Navigate directly into a subroutine, include, and function module by double-clicking on the object name in the editor.

▸ By double-clicking on the variable name, navigate to the data declaration part of that variable.

▸ Navigate to each respective element by double-clicking on the table, structure, and data element definitions name in the editor.

▸ Navigate to all subobjects displayed hierarchically in the object tree on the left side.

▸ Navigate to the other objects by writing their names directly into the Object Name field on the left side.

All navigation steps are recorded in the Navigation Stack tool while you're navigating within the Object Navigator. You can always go back and forth between navigation steps until you navigate to a new step. All forward steps are cleared at that point, and the Navigation Stack tool continues with the new path.

Let's see this in an example. Start the Object Navigator with Transaction SE80 and perform the following steps:

1. Open ABAP program BCALV_GRID_01.
2. Navigate to a line where the `popup_to_inform` function is called, and double-click on the function name. You have now navigated into the function module.
3. Open ABAP program BCALV_GRID_02 by manually entering its name in the Object name field.
4. Double-click on the method definition `handle_double_click`, and navigate into the method implementation.
5. Find the line where `gt_sbook` is declared, and double-click on it to navigate to its definition.
6. Double-click on the SBOOK table that is used in the declaration part, and open the table definition.
7. Double-click on the data element S_CARR_ID of column CARRID.
8. Double-click on the domain S_CARR_ID.

Now, all of these steps have been recorded in the Navigation Stack tool, and you can navigate to any of these steps easily. To do this, open the Navigation Stack window by choosing Utilities • Display Navigation Window.

You can see all of the steps you just performed in the Navigation Stack tool as shown in Figure 1.

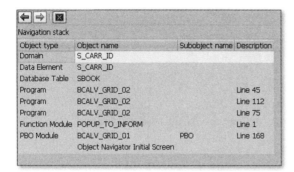

≪ Figure 1 *Navigation Stack Items*

Use the arrow buttons at the top of the screen to navigate back and forth within the list. Alternatively, double-click on any of these steps to navigate to it.

Note that the Navigation Stack tool stores data for each session but clears data immediately when you exit the Object Navigator.

Tip **4**

Inserting Statement Patterns in ABAP Programs with Drag and Drop

When working on ABAP programs, you can insert statement patterns by dragging relevant entries from the object tree to the ABAP Editor to avoid making manual mistakes.

Some statement patterns can be very difficult to remember, and you're likely to make a mistake if you try to write a full statement manually. Instead, you can drag the relevant object from the object list into the ABAP Editor to create a source code pattern to use that object in your ABAP program. This feature is extremely useful for complex statement patterns.

✓ And Here's How ...

When you open a development object in the Object Navigator, you can see all of the subobjects in a hierarchical tree. You can create the following statements by dragging the relevant object from the Object Navigator and dropping it into the ABAP Editor:

- ▶ Instantiate global class
- ▶ Call method of global class
- ▶ Call function module
- ▶ Call subroutine

You can also drag and drop these objects from your worklist.

Perform the following steps to insert a statement pattern into the editor:

1. Open an ABAP program in the Object Navigator.

2. In the navigation area, select the object that you want to create a statement for in the editor by clicking on it.

3. Drag the object name and drop it into the editor as shown in Figure 1.

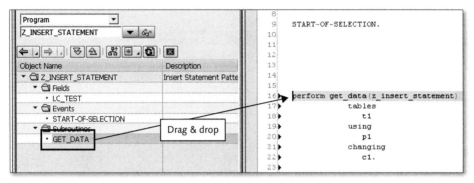

⌃ **Figure 1** *Dragging and Dropping an Object into the ABAP Editor*

4. Optional parameters of methods and function modules are commented by default. Uncomment them if you're going to use these parameters.

Figure 2 shows the program statements that are generated with drag and drop.

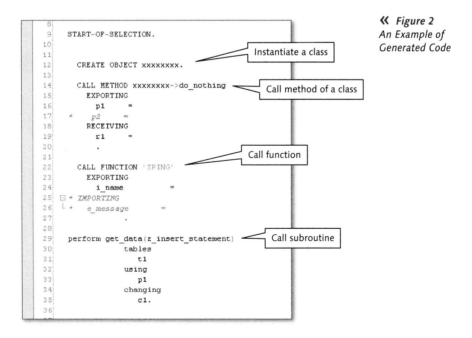

《 *Figure 2*
An Example of
Generated Code

You can adjust insert pattern settings. You can also modify the code generation settings for function modules and classes according to your programming style by choosing UTILITIES • SETTINGS.

Select the PATTRN tab within the ABAP EDITOR tab. Figure 3 shows the settings that you can adjust.

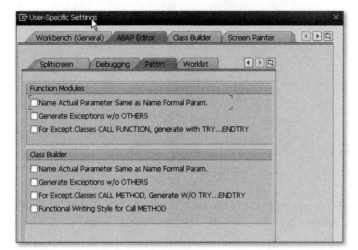

《 Figure 3 *Settings Window*

Tip 5

Using Worklists to Group Development Objects

You can add development objects and navigation targets into your worklist for future use so you don't have to waste time searching for them.

A worklist allows you to mark an object or specific place in an object for later retrieval. It's similar to a bookmark system that allows you to store and organize your most commonly used development objects together and navigate to them easily in the future. Unlike a favorites or bookmarks list, however, worklists allow you to save the same object several times with different source code positions. This feature allows you to set markers for later use in the source code. Now, let's see how you can add objects to a worklist.

✓ And Here's How ...

To add a particular development object into your worklist, open it in its editor and select the menu option:

UTILITIES • WORKLIST • INSERT CURRENT OBJECT

If you add an ABAP program, function module, or class library, the worklist also stores the current position in the source code. You can add the same program multiple times with different positions in the source code. This feature allows you to set markers in your programs. You can get back to that position anytime you want.

To display the objects in your worklist, select the following menu path while editing an object in the Object Navigator or a different appropriate tool:

UTILITIES • WORKLIST • DISPLAY

The DISPLAY WORKLIST window opens at the bottom of the window as shown in Figure 1. Here you can see existing objects in your worklist.

Object type	Object name	Subobject name	Source code	Comment
Function Module	Z_PING		10	
Method	ZCL_TEST	DO_NOTHING	2	You can add your comments
Program	Z_INSERT_STATEMENT		9	
Program	Z_INSERT_STATEMENT		25	Call Function
Program	Z_INSERT_STATEMENT		44	Form do_nothing

⌃ *Figure 1* *A Worklist with Sample Data*

You can also add your comments for worklist items as shown in the figure. This is especially useful if you add the different source code positions of the same object many times into the worklist. It would be difficult to distinguish between the worklist items belonging to the same object by only looking at the source code line.

You can use the following functions on the toolbar to maintain the worklist items:

▶ SAVE WORKLIST (🖫)
Saves the worklist. Worklist items are not saved into the database by default. The list is cleared when you exit from the editor. You have to manually save the worklist using this function to be able to use the same worklist later.

▶ DELETE OBJECT FROM WORKLIST (🗏)
Deletes the selected object from the worklist.

▶ INSERT CURRENT OBJECT INTO WORKLIST (🗏)
Inserts the currently open object into the worklist.

▶ DELETE ENTIRE WORKLIST (🗑)
Empties the worklist. It also deletes all worklist items from the database.

▶ RELOAD WORKLIST FROM DATABASE (🔁)
Discards your changes that have been in the current session or after the last save and reloads the worklist items from the database.

Managing Your Frequently Used Objects with a Favorites List

You can add frequently used development objects into your favorites list so you can find them easily in the future.

The Object Navigator allows you to work on several types of development objects, including package, program, function group, class, and interface. You can create, modify, or display any of these objects by selecting the appropriate object type and writing the object name into the relevant field. When you're working in the Object Navigator, you can add frequently used development objects into your favorites list to find them easily later.

And Here's How ...

The Object Navigator has a user-specific favorites list that allows you to store frequently used development objects. Later, you can navigate to these objects easily by selecting them from the favorites list. This list can be especially helpful when you're working on a project that requires you to work on several types of development objects within different packages.

To add an object into your favorites list, open it in the Object Navigator and click the ADD button on the toolbar as shown in Figure 1.

《 Figure 1 *Adding an Object to Favorites*

You can also edit your favorites list by clicking the EDIT link in the same menu. The EDIT FAVORITES window opens as shown in Figure 2.

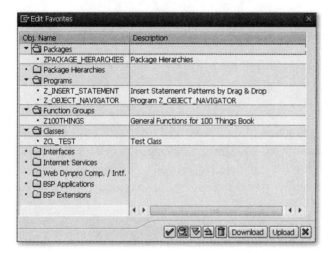

《 Figure 2 *Edit Favorites*

You can use the following functions on the EDIT FAVORITES window:

▶ DELETE
Deletes the selected object from the favorites list.

▶ DOWNLOAD
Allows you to download the favorites list to transfer between the systems.

▶ UPLOAD
Allows you to upload previously saved favorites lists. The system triggers a popup to ask you whether you want to replace the old favorites list with the new one or append the new items into the list by keeping the old items.

Finally, you can use your favorites list to navigate your frequently used objects easily by selecting it from the favorites list as shown in Figure 3.

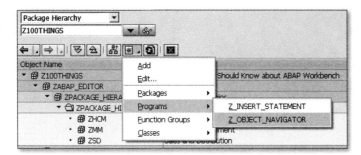

« *Figure 3* *Navigating to the Development Object from the Favorites List*

Tip 7

Comparing ABAP Programs between Two Systems

You can compare ABAP programs in different systems to find potential errors or inconsistencies in the code.

Sometimes you may want to compare ABAP programs between two different systems to find a problem that might occur due to different patch levels, or to find an old request that was transported by mistake. To accomplish this, we'll show you how to use the Remote Comparison in Version Management tool when you see a problem in an ABAP program and want to make sure it's identical to another system.

✓ And Here's How ...

When you're editing an ABAP program, you can view the Version Management tool by selecting the following menu path:

UTILITIES • VERSIONS • VERSION MANAGEMENT

You can see the previous versions of the program you were working on as shown in Figure 1.

To start the Remote Comparison tool, click REMOTE COMPARISON on the toolbar. You'll see two options to define a remote SAP system. If the SAP system you want to compare is configured in the transport management system, you can select the SAP system directly. Otherwise, you have to create an RFC destination for a remote system.

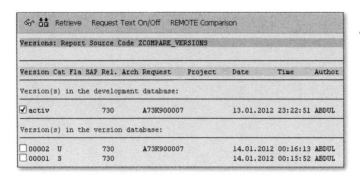

« *Figure 1* Version Management

When you click REMOTE COMPARISON, versions of the same ABAP program in a remote system are displayed. You can select any of the remote versions and click REMOTE COMPARISON. The COMPARE PROGRAMS screen opens as shown in Figure 2 and displays two versions at the same time with highlighted differences.

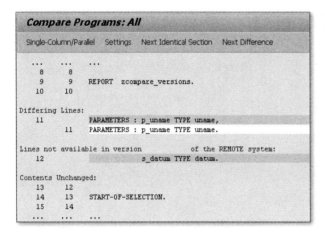

« *Figure 2* Compare Programs Screen

You can click on NEXT IDENTICAL SECTION and NEXT DIFFERENCE in the toolbar to navigate through source code to analyze the differences. You can open the SETTINGS window and adjust the display settings by clicking on SETTINGS on the toolbar. The following options are available:

▶ Switch between SINGLE-COLUMN DISPLAY, PARALLEL DISPLAY, and DISPLAY IN SPLITSCREEN EDITOR

▶ Switch between DISPLAY ALL, MATCHES CONDENSED, and DISPLAY DIFFERENCES ONLY

▶ DISPLAY LINE NUMBERING

- IGNORE INDENTATIONS
- IGNORE COMMENTS

You can adjust these options to use the different features of the tool to easily display the differences between two ABAP programs.

Modifying and Testing Programs with Inactive Versions of Development Objects

You can modify and test development objects in your local runtime environment without affecting other users and objects in your system.

Say you need to make a change in a development object, but other users might be using this object on the same system while you're editing it. How do you make changes without booting users from the system or modifying an object that is currently in use?

The ABAP Workbench contains a feature that allows you to modify and test development objects in your local runtime system while other users use the active version of the program. In this tip, we'll show you how to use this feature so when you're sure that changes are finished and working correctly, you can activate the object to commit the changes to the system.

✓ And Here's How ...

Development objects appear in the following statuses at different times within the development lifecycle:

- ▶ New (Revised)
- ▶ New
- ▶ Inactive
- ▶ Inactive (Revised)

▶ Active (Revised)

▶ Active

When you create a new development object, it takes the status of New (Revised) or Inactive, depending on the type. For example, an SAP ABAP Data Dictionary object takes the status New (Revised) immediately after you create it. On the other hand, a program or function module takes the status Inactive.

Figure 1 shows all possible combinations of the status changes during the development process.

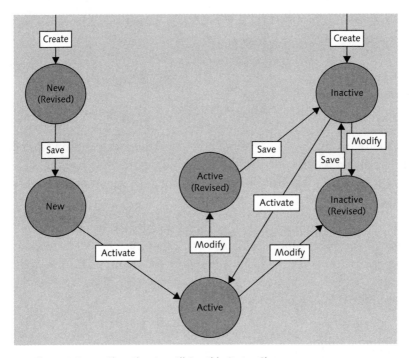

⌃ *Figure 1* *Status Flow Showing All Possible Status Changes*

When you start to modify a development object, it takes the status Inactive, and the global runtime system isn't affected with these changes. It's visible only to you until you manually activate the object. Other users can only use the active version of the object and they can't see your changes until you activate the object. All inactive objects are included in your *Inactive Objects list*. You can access your inactive objects list by selecting ENVIRONMENT • INACTIVE OBJECTS in the Object Navigator (see Figure 2).

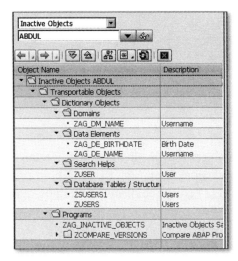

« **Figure 2** *Inactive Objects List*

When another user tries to modify any of these objects, the system generates a new task for that user in the same transport request and adds the object into the user's Inactive Objects list. Now both users can see the same object in their Inactive Object list. Let's see an example:

- ▶ User A changes the following objects and leaves them inactive:
  - ▶ Program Z_PROG_1
  - ▶ Program Z_PROG_2
  - ▶ Table Z_TABLE_1
- ▶ User B changes the following objects and leaves them inactive:
  - ▶ Program Z_PROG_2
  - ▶ Program Z_PROG_3
  - ▶ Table Z_TABLE_1

User A and B are working on Program Z_PROG_2 and Table Z_TABLE_1 together. They are also modifying other listed programs individually. Table 1 shows the runtime environment for the users after these changes.

Local Runtime Environment – User A	Local Runtime Environment – User B	Global Runtime Environment
Z_PROG_1 (Inactive)	Z_PROG_1 (Active)	Z_PROG_1 (Active)
Z_PROG_2 (Inactive)	Z_PROG_2 (Inactive)	Z_PROG_2 (Active)
Z_PROG_3 (Active)	Z_PROG_3 (Inactive)	Z_PROG_3 (Active)
Z_TABLE_1 (Inactive)	Z_TABLE_1 (Inactive)	Z_TABLE_1 (Active)

⌃ *Table 1* Differences on Local Runtime Environments for User A, User B, and the Global Runtime Environment

As you can see, users only see the inactive object if it's included in their Inactive Objects list; otherwise they see the active version. User A and User B both can see the inactive version of Program Z_PROG_2 because they are working on that program together.

Creating Local Objects for Test Purposes

You can create development objects that will be used only for test or experimental purposes.

The package concept in the ABAP Workbench allows you to group development objects into separate packages depending on their usage, as discussed in Tip 1. However, if you want to create an object for test purposes only, and you aren't planning to transport it to another system, you can create the object as a local object.

 And Here's How ...

If you're creating an object for test or experimental purposes, you don't need to assign the development object to a package during creation. Click the LOCAL OBJECT button on the popup dialog as shown in Figure 1 to create the object as a local object. You can also assign the development object to the package $TMP for the same purpose.

In the Object Navigator (Transaction SE80), you can see the hierarchical list of local objects belonging to any user by selecting LOCAL OBJECT as the object type and entering the username in the OBJECT name field as shown in Figure 2.

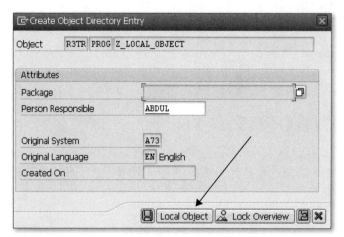

《 Figure 1 *Package Assignment Dialog*

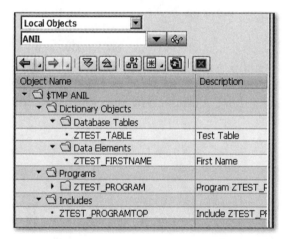

《 Figure 2 *Hierarchical List of Local Objects*

Local objects are used mainly for test purposes and can't be transported to other SAP systems. If you want to transport local objects, assign them to another package. Package assignment can be changed by selecting the object name from the object list by choosing OTHER FUNCTIONS • CHANGE in the context menu.

Tip 10

Creating and Accessing Documentation for Development Objects

You can create technical documentation for development objects directly in the SAP system.

Preparing good technical documentation is one of the most important stages of development projects—there should always be technical documentation to describe the functionality and architecture of the developed program. For example, when you're required to modify a program that you or someone else developed a long time ago, you'll probably need to read the documentation of the program before modifying the source code. However, it isn't always easy to find the technical specifications of the programs after a while. In this tip, we'll show you how to create brief technical documentations for development objects directly in the SAP system to make it easier to find and update.

✅ And Here's How ...

When you open a development object for editing, select GOTO • DOCUMENTATION in the menu. A screen opens where you can edit documentation for the object. There are two types of editors that you can use:

- **Graphical PC Editor**
  Here you can input your text continuously. After SAP NetWeaver 7.0 EHP1 or 7.1 SP05 versions, Microsoft Word was integrated into the Graphical PC Editor, which makes it a lot easier to use. The Graphical PC Editor is much easier to use than the Line Editor.

▶ **Line Editor**

This old-style editor in the SAP system has been replaced by the Graphical PC Editor, which is much more user friendly. Here you'll find a format column where you specify the paragraph formats or format commands. The text entry part is built from separate 72-character input text fields for each line.

Figure 1 shows the screenshots of the different types of editors.

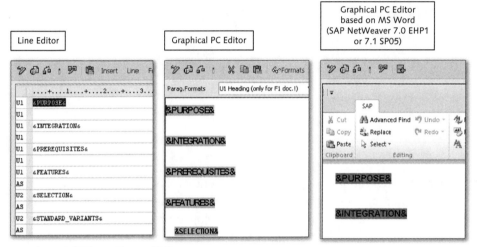

⌃ *Figure 1 Different Types of Editors*

You can switch between the editors by choosing GOTO • CHANGE EDITOR while you're in the editor.

Let's create sample documentation for a custom program to see the steps involved:

1. Open the ABAP program that you want to create documentation for in the ABAP Editor in change mode, and select GOTO • DOCUMENTATION in the menu. When you open documentation of an object for the first time, the system proposes a template where you can enter the documentation of the program. It's separated by headers to let you organize the documentation into groups such as purpose, functionality, and integration. After you finish providing enough details for each part, you can save the documentation, and it will be available to all users on the system.

2. To open the ABAP program in display mode, use GOTO • DOCUMENTATION. Figure 2 shows example documentation.

```
 Display Documentation:




FU REUSE_ALV_GRID_DISPLAY
_____


Short Text

    Output of a simple list (single-line)

  Functionality

    The function module outputs an internal table with whatever structure in
    the form of a formatted single- oder multi-line list.



  Process:

    o   Passing an internal table with the set of information to be output

    o   Passing a structure with general layout specifications for list
        layout

    o   Passing a field catalog in the form of an internal table
```

⌃ **Figure 2** *Documentation for Function Module REUSE_ALV_GRID_DISPLAY*

Creating a documentation using this technique is fairly easy but can be very useful in the future. You don't need to provide much technical details; only a brief documentation will be enough. Both end users and developers can use these documentations in the future to get information about the object.

Tip 11

Reserving Namespaces with SAP for Third-Party Objects

When you plan to develop software that will be delivered to third parties, you can reserve your own namespace from SAP to eliminate the risk of name conflicts.

Customer objects in the SAP system can only start with Y or Z. All other letters can only be used by SAP. In SAP projects, it's very common to prepare naming standards for objects before starting the project to minimize the risk of name conflicts. However, when you develop software that will be delivered to third parties, you have to make sure that there are no objects on the target system that have the same name as any of your objects. SAP allows you to reserve your own namespace to eliminate the risk of name conflicts for these types of developments, and we'll show you how this is done.

✓ And Here's How ...

Your company must have the ABAP/4 Development Workbench license to be able to reserve a namespace. If your company has the required license, you can apply for a namespace through *http://service.sap.com/namespaces*. Figure 1 shows the namespace reservation screen from the SAP Support Portal.

You must provide the following information:

- ▶ Name for namespace
  - ▶ The name must be a minimum of three and a maximum of eight characters
  - ▶ You can't use spaces or special characters in the name
  - ▶ The name must clearly refer to the name of the company

- ▶ The name can't start with a number, "SAP", or "R3" character strings
- ▶ The "/" character is automatically added to the beginning and end of the name
▶ Intended purpose to reserve a namespace
▶ The installation numbers of the systems to use the requested namespace

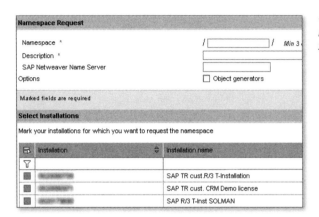

« Figure 1 *Namespace Reservation through SAP Support Portal*

After you receive the authorization to retrieve the namespace, you can obtain the namespace license keys from the SAP Support Portal. Then you must set up the namespace within your own system with the following procedure:

1. Go to Transaction SE03 to open Transport Organizer Tools.
2. Select DISPLAY/CHANGE NAMESPACES in the ADMINISTRATION node.
3. Click the DISPLAY -> CHANGE button on the toolbar to switch to change mode.
4. Click the NEW ENTRIES button on the toolbar to enter the details of the new namespace.
5. Fill in the details.

You can create two types of namespace entries in this way:

▶ PRODUCER
Choose this type if you are the owner of the namespace and have the valid development license.

▶ RECIPIENT
Choose this type if you want to make changes on the objects that are delivered to you with a special namespace and have the valid repair license.

Repair licenses are not installation specific and can be delivered by the namespace owner to enable the delivered objects to be repaired.

Tip 12

Using the Application Hierarchy Tool to Organize Applications

You can navigate through all standard and custom applications in a hierarchical list, as well as create your own to categorize your packages.

The ABAP Workbench has several tools such as *packages* and *package hierarchies* that allow you to organize development objects. The Application Hierarchy tool allows you to categorize and navigate through objects at a higher level; it basically helps you to create a catalog for your applications within the SAP system. You can browse through the application hierarchy to find a package when you know the application that it belongs to, but you don't know the technical name. You can also create your own hierarchy for custom packages to allow other developers to find the package easily in the future, which we'll discuss in this tip.

✓ And Here's How ...

There are two types of application hierarchies in the ABAP Workbench:

► **SAP**
All SAP packages are organized in this hierarchy by application components. You can browse through the SAP Application Hierarchy to find out the standard applications delivered in your SAP system.

► **Custom**
You can't add your custom applications into the SAP Application Hierarchy. Instead, you can create a custom application hierarchy for your custom packages to catalog your applications. You can also include SAP packages in a custom application hierarchy.

You can access SAP and custom hierarchies in the following menu option in the Object Navigator:

ENVIRONMENT • APPLICATION HIERARCHY

You can also use Transaction SE81 for SAP and Transaction SE82 for customer hierarchies. Figure 1 shows the Application Hierarchy for SAP objects.

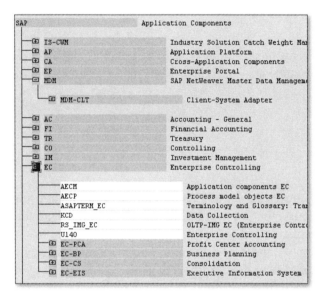

« Figure 1 Application Hierarchy for SAP Applications

There are two types of nodes in the Application Hierarchy tool:

- Title node
- Development node

When you create a node, it's created as a title node automatically. Title nodes are used like folders, and they help you create multi-level hierarchies. After you assign a package to a node, it becomes a development node. You can navigate to a package directly from the Application Hierarchy tool by clicking on development nodes.

Tip **13**

Searching for Objects in Transport Requests with Transport Organizer Tools

When you have a lot of transport requests in your system, there's a tool you can use to quickly and easily search for specific transport requests that contain a specific development object.

When you create and modify development objects in ABAP Workbench, the SAP system creates a transport request for you to organize your changes. Changes that belong to the same task are usually put into the same transport request. When there are many transport requests, it can be difficult to find the transport request for an object. We'll show you how to use Transport Organizer Tools to help you find a specific transport request in this situation.

☑ And Here's How ...

The Transport Organizer Tool contains tools that help you with issues related to change and transport management system, and they can be accessed via Transaction SE03. In Transport Organizer Tools, you can use the SEARCH FOR OBJECTS IN REQUESTS/TASKS application to find the transport request for a particular object. Figure 1 shows the initial view of the application.

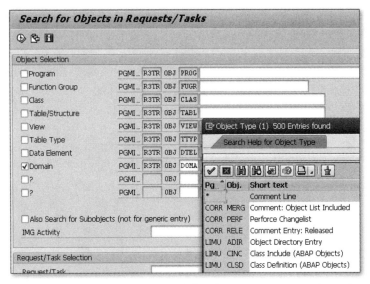

⌃ *Figure 1* *Initial View of the Search for Objects in Requests/Tasks Application*

You can choose from predefined object types or select any other object type using the search help. If you made your changes in Customizing and don't know which object is used in the IMG activity, you can search by selecting the relevant IMG ACTIVITY. It's also possible to filter the results with the following selection parameters:

- ▸ REQUEST/TASK NUMBER
- ▸ REQUEST OWNER
- ▸ REQUEST DATE
- ▸ REQUEST STATUS (MODIFIABLE/RELEASED)
- ▸ REQUEST TYPE

When you execute the application after specifying the selection parameters, the system lists all of the requests and tasks separately. You can also navigate to the request/task from the result screen by double-clicking on its name.

Let's consider an example to show how you can use this tool. Suppose that you want to see the transport requests of all changes in the contents of Table ZAG_TEST for a selected time interval in the system.

Select R3TR TABU ZAG_TEST in the OBJECT SELECTION part of the SEARCH FOR OBJECTS IN REQUESTS/TASKS SCREEN. On the selection screen, you can't change the object type of the predefined objects. If you want to select another object type rather than the predefined object types, as in our case, you can use the last three object types in the list. Note that you can't select program ID R3TR manually; instead you just select TABU and press ⌊Enter⌋. R3TR is automatically filled in on the field. You can also specify a table range in the DATE field. Finally, the selection screen must be like the one shown in Figure 2.

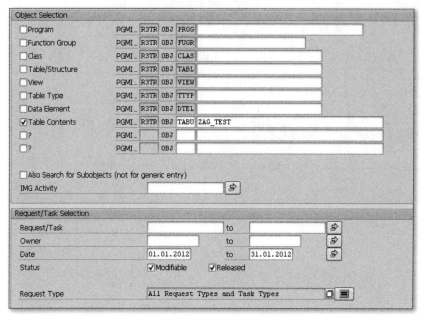

≽ **Figure 2** *Filling in the Selection Screen to Find the Changes in Table ZAG_TEST*

When you execute the report, the results are displayed as shown in Figure 3.

Request	Short Description	Owner	Date	Type	Status
A73K900022	Ticket Number : 14543345	ABDUL	06.01.2012	Customizing Request	Released
A73K900023	asdf	ABDUL	06.01.2012	Customizing Task	Released
A73K900025	Table Changes	ANIL	06.01.2012	Customizing Request	Released
A73K900026	Table Changes	ANIL	06.01.2012	Customizing Task	Released
A73K900028	Test Results	ANIL	06.01.2012	Customizing Task	Modif.

≽ **Figure 3** *List of Requests That Changes the Contents of Table ZAG_TEST*

You can use other options on the selection screen to filter the results even more. You can search the transport requests for all types of objects in the ABAP Workbench. Note that this example is especially useful when you want to audit the changes on the critical objects in the system.

Searching for Development Objects using the Repository Information System

Instead of struggling with different tools for different objects, you can use the Repository Information System to search all types of objects in the SAP system.

The SAP system allows you to create several types of development objects. However, when you're looking for a development object and you want to perform a detailed search, using specific selection criteria, it can be difficult to use different tools for each type of object. To bypass this issue, we'll show you how to use the *Repository Information System* as a central point to search through all types of development objects or find the objects that use a particular object (where-used list).

✓ And Here's How ...

You can access the Repository Information System with Transaction SE84 or by choosing ENVIRONMENT • REPOSITORY INFORMATION SYSTEM in the Object Navigator.

All development objects are organized hierarchically as shown in Figure 1.

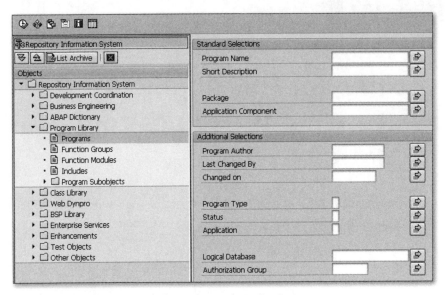

You can navigate through the hierarchy in Figure 1 to find the object type that you want to search, and then double-click to open the selection screen specific to the selected object type. Each selection screen has object-specific parameters. The selection screen has two parts: STANDARD SELECTIONS and ADDITIONAL SELECTIONS. Initially, ADDITIONAL SELECTIONS criteria are hidden and can be opened by clicking on the ALL SELECTIONS button (⊞) on the toolbar if you want to provide more details for the selection. You can also change the initial variant to show ALL SELECTIONS criteria by using the SETTINGS button on the toolbar or clicking EDIT • SETTINGS.

There are also default variants for some object types that help make your searches easier. For example, open the selection screen for FUNCTION MODULES below the node PROGRAM LIBRARY, and get the list of variants using the GET VARIANT button (📁) on the toolbar. You can see that there are predefined variants to search for a BAPI or RFC functions.

You can also use the Repository Information System to get where-used lists for development objects to find which objects use this object.

Where-Used List

You can start the Where-Used List tool on the Repository Information System by right-clicking on the object type in the object tree and selecting the WHERE-USED LIST item from the context menu. A popup opens and displays the selection criteria screen specific to the selected object type. You can enter the object name and select the object types in which the system should make a search. After you click EXECUTE, the system lists the objects that use the selected object as shown in Figure 2.

Table Fields	Short Description
/OSP/T_REPMD5BKT	OSP : Report MD5 Book Keeping Table
☐ USERID	User Name in User Master Record
/OSP/T_TEAMD5BKT	OSP : Team Management MD5 Book Keeping Table
☐ USERID	User Name in User Master Record
/SAPPO/USER	User(s) for Cross-System Tasks
☐ BNAME	User Name in User Master Record
/SAPTRX/CONF_EHO	EH display configuration- overview screen
☐ TAB_USER	User Name in User Master Record
/SAPTRX/SOSCUSR	Scenario User Mapping Table
☐ UNAME	User Name in User Master Record

≫ *Figure 2* *Where-Used List of an Object*

Environment Analysis

Another useful tool in the Repository Information System is Environment Analysis, which allows you to see the encapsulation of an object by listing the external object references.

You can start the Environment Analysis tool by right-clicking on an object type in the Repository Information System and selecting ENVIRONMENT ANALYSIS from the context menu. It's used to list the external objects that are used in the selected object. For example, you can list all external object references (function modules, tables, etc.) in an ABAP program before transporting it to another system. The results are displayed in a list sorted by packages. You'll then use this list to ensure that all of these used objects exist in the target system.

Tip 15

Using OO Transactions to Link Class Methods to Transaction Codes

You can create a transaction code linked to a public method of a class that's defined either in an ABAP program or the Class Builder.

The object-oriented (OO) programming model in ABAP Workbench has significantly changed how we design and develop ABAP programs. In addition to classical programming methods, you can now define an ABAP object in the Class Builder or in an ABAP program. This change has also caused a new requirement to link transaction codes directly to the methods of classes. We'll show you how to create and use OO transactions to fulfill this requirement.

✓ And Here's How ...

OO transactions are used to assign a transaction code to class methods. You can create an OO transaction by performing the following steps:

1. Go to Transaction SE93.
2. Enter the transaction code you want to link to, and click the CREATE button.
3. Enter the SHORT TEXT, and select METHOD OF A CLASS in START OBJECT group.
4. Enter the name of the class in the CLASS NAME field.
5. Enter any public method of the class (note that search help isn't available here). The method can't have any mandatory import parameters.
6. Select OO TRANSACTION MODEL if you're using an instance method and want to use the OO transaction model.

If you're calling an instance method, the system automatically generates an instance of the class in an internal session. The constructor method of the class must be public and can't have any mandatory import parameters because it's called during the initialization.

To illustrate how to use the OO transaction, let's go over the demo Program DEMO_OO_TRANSACTION and Transaction DEMO_OO_METHOD that exist in the SAP system. As you can see in the following code, there is only a class definition and implementation in the program:

```
PROGRAM  demo_oo_transaction.

CLASS demo_class DEFINITION.
  PUBLIC SECTION.
    METHODS instance_method.
ENDCLASS.

CLASS demo_class IMPLEMENTATION.
  METHOD instance_method.
    MESSAGE 'Instance method in local class' TYPE 'I'.
  ENDMETHOD.
ENDCLASS.
```

You can't run the program with direct processing (F8) because the program type is SUBROUTINE POOL. There isn't any EVENT BLOCK in the program; therefore, nothing would change even if you switched the program type to EXECUTABLE PROGRAM.

Assigning an OO transaction is the only option to run this program. Access Transaction SE93 to see the details of the demo Transaction DEMO_OO_METHOD. As you can see in Figure 1, it links the method INSTANCE_METHOD of class DEMO_CLASS to the transaction code DEMO_OO_METHOD.

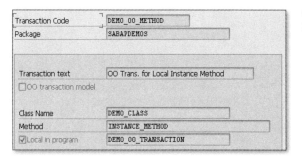

« *Figure 1* *An Example of the OO Transaction*

Now the OO transaction is assigned to the local class defined in an ABAP program. You can also assign the OO transaction to the instance or static methods of the classes defined in Class Builder.

OO transactions are useful when you develop an ABAP program using an OO programming model. You don't have to use event blocks such as `Start-of-selection` or assign a transaction code to a program. You can directly implement a class and assign the transaction code to the methods of this class. You can even create separate transactions for different methods of the same class.

Tip (16)

Using Forward Navigation to Create Objects

You can create objects, data elements, and domains in the ABAP Workbench without ever having to leave the development tool.

When you're editing a development object in the ABAP Workbench, you usually need to work with several types of development objects at the same time. The forward navigation feature in the ABAP Workbench allows you to navigate to an object by double-clicking on the object name. The system automatically opens the object in the relevant development tool. Several types of objects can be opened using this method.

Without this feature, it would be frustrating having to navigate between the tools or opening new SAP GUI session for each development tool. In this tip, we'll show how you can use forward navigation feature to create development objects in the same window without leaving the tool or opening another session.

✓ And Here's How ...

If you want to use an object that doesn't exist in the ABAP Workbench while you write code in the ABAP Editor, you can write the object name to be created and double-click the object name. The system will tell you that the object doesn't exist and ask whether you want to create the object.

As an example, if you want to create a subroutine called `get_data` in your program, instead of navigating to the suitable source code position and manually write the code for the subroutine, you can write the command `PERFORM get_data` and double-click on `get_data`. The popup appears as shown in Figure 1; create the object by clicking YES.

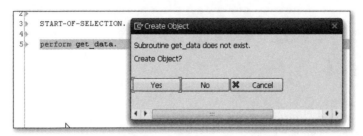

⌃ *Figure 1 Create a Subroutine Using Forward Navigation*

This rule isn't valid just in the ABAP Editor. You can also create different repository objects (classes, tables, structures, data elements, search helps, etc.) in any of the tools in the ABAP Workbench.

One of the most common usages of this feature is CREATING data elements and domains while creating a new table. If this feature weren't available, you would have to perform the following tasks for all fields of the tables:

1. Create domain.

2. Create data element.

3. Add a new field to a table, and assign the created data element.

However, if you use forward navigation, you just have to follow these steps to create a new data element and domain while creating a new field in the table:

1. Add a new field to a table assign a data element that doesn't exist yet.

2. Double-click on the data element to create it.

3. Assign a domain to a data element that doesn't exist yet.

4. Double-click on the domain to create.

5. Go back twice to add a new field.

The benefit of using this method is that you never leave the Create Table tool. You're able to create all data elements and domains in the same window without leaving the tool.

Tip (17)

Uploading/Downloading User-Specific Settings to a Different System

You can download user-specific settings from one system and upload to another system to create duplicate environments or restore your settings.

You can use the USER-SPECIFIC SETTINGS window to adjust settings that you use in the ABAP Workbench. Settings options are included for almost all of the ABAP Workbench tools. However, if you work on multiple systems, it can be difficult to keep the settings in all systems synchronized and use the same settings everywhere. UPLOAD and DOWNLOAD functions allow you to back up your settings or restore them to any system you want.

✓ And Here's How ...

Open the USER-SPECIFIC SETTINGS window by choosing UTILITIES • SETTINGS while you're in the Object Navigator. As you can see in Figure 1, you can adjust settings for almost all ABAP Workbench tools.

These settings allow you to customize several features of all ABAP Workbench tools to create a comfortable environment according to your preferences.

After working in a specific SAP system, you may not even remember which settings you've changed when you move to another system. So when you start to use ABAP Workbench tools on another SAP system, you'll immediately notice that you need to change the user-specific settings again according your preferences to use the tools more efficiently. You can then go to your old system and open the USER-

SPECIFIC SETTINGS window (as described at the beginning of the tip) and use the
DOWNLOAD button on the popup toolbar to download your custom settings. After
providing the location and file name, settings are saved in a file in your file system.
You even can make simple modifications to this text file using any text editor.

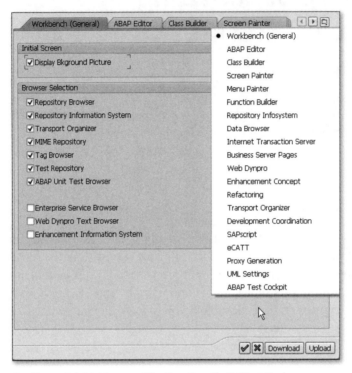

⌃ *Figure 1 Initial Screen of the User-Specific Settings Tool*

You can now log on to the new system and open the USER-SPECIFIC SETTINGS
window again. This time, click the UPLOAD button and select the file you saved in
the previous step. Finally, all settings are restored to the new system from your
previous system.

Using Package Interfaces to Create a Set of Visible Development Objects

You can create programming interfaces for your package and also define which development objects can be used by others.

The packaging concept in SAP systems allows you to put all development objects belonging to the same application together in the same package. When you create a package for your application, all objects in the package are encapsulated from other packages by default to protect the use of these objects from other packages. However, you might also need to use the development objects from other packages, or other packages might need to use an object from your package. In this tip, you'll learn how to create package interfaces and expose development objects through these interfaces to allow other packages to use these objects.

✓ And Here's How ...

Let's explore a scenario where you've created the following development objects and want to open them for use in more than one program:

▶ Function Module Z_PING in Package ZPI1

▶ Program ZPI_TEST in Package ZPI2

When you call the Z_PING function module from the ZPI_TEST program and perform a syntax check, you'll get a message as shown in Figure 1.

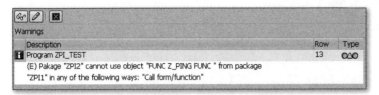

⊼ *Figure 1* Syntax Check Result When You Call a Function Module from a Different Package

This message indicates that you must perform the following tasks to be able to use the Z_PING function module in the ZPI_TEST program:

1. Create a package interface in Package ZPI1.
2. Expose the Z_PING function module in a package interface.
3. Add the created package interface into the dependency control list of Package ZPI2.

Let's perform these tasks step by step:

1. Create an interface for Package ZPI1 by right-clicking on a package in Transaction SE80 and selecting the following item from the context menu:

CREATE • DEVELOPMENT COORDINATION • PACKAGE INTERFACE

2. After providing the name and description of the package interface in the popup dialog, the package interface maintenance screen is displayed. Navigate to the EXPOSED OBJECTS tab, and drag Function Module Z_PING from the object list into the EXPOSED OBJECT area on the right side. The result should be as shown in Figure 2.

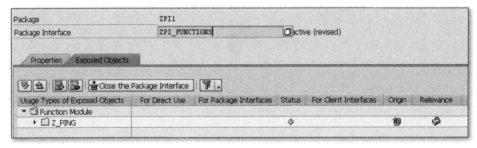

⊼ *Figure 2* Exposed Objects List of Package Interface

3. Save and activate the package interface to finish the process. You can now insert the created package interface into the dependency control list of Package ZPI2.

4. Open Package ZPI2 in the Object Navigator, and double-click on the package name to open the package maintenance screen.

5. Navigate to the DEPENDENCY CONTROL LIST tab, and click on the ADD button (⬜ Add) to start adding the created package into the list. A popup dialog opens and fills in the values as shown in Figure 3.

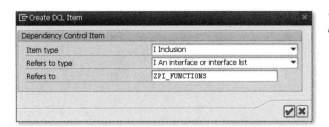

« *Figure 3 Creating a Dependency for a Package*

6. Click the CONTINUE (✓) to add the package interface into the dependency control list. Save and activate the package to finish the process.

7. Finally, repeat the syntax check on Program ZPI_TEST to see that there isn't any message.

As shown in the example, package interfaces help you create programming interfaces for your packages. Other packages are able to use only the objects in these interfaces. You'll then prevent the problems that might arise due to using the wrong objects from other packages by proposing the object list that other people can use from your package.

Part 2

ABAP Editor

Things You'll Learn in this Section

The ABAP Editor is one of the most important tools in ABAP Workbench, helping you to create and maintain ABAP programs. When you're developing an ABAP program, you need more than a tool that only lets you write your programs line by line. A modern programming editor must have tools that provide practical and time-saving features to allow developers to write their code efficiently. The ABAP Editor accordingly comes with several features that increase your productivity. In this part of the book, you'll learn tips and tricks that will help you use the tool more efficiently.

Tip (19)

Comparing ABAP Programs with the Splitscreen Editor

You can use the Splitscreen Editor to view the source code of two ABAP programs on the same screen with special comparison functions.

When you're displaying or editing source code in the ABAP Editor, you may need to compare the current program with another, either on the same system or a different system. The classical method is to open the program in a new window, but you can't easily see the difference between the programs while they are in different windows. Alternatively, you can open two programs in the *Splitscreen Editor,* which allows you to view, modify, or compare the source code of two ABAP programs, function modules, or classes on the same screen with special comparison functions.

✓ And Here's How ...

First, access the Splitscreen Editor with Transaction SE39. As shown in Figure 1, enter two program names in the respective LEFT-JUSTIFIED and RIGHT sections on the selection screen. Click the DISPLAY button, and the two programs will appear, side by side.

⊼ **Figure 1** *Initial Screen of the Splitscreen Editor*

You can also compare programs on different systems; for example, programs on development and quality systems. To do this, click the COMPARE DIFFERENT SYSTEMS button on the toolbar in Figure 1. Now a new field called RFC DESTINATION shows up at the bottom of the selection screen where you can enter your selection (see Figure 2).

⊼ **Figure 2** *RFC Destination Field to Compare Different Systems*

Note that you can only open the programs in display mode when you're comparing programs on different systems.

After you click the DISPLAY or CHANGE button, two programs are opened on the same screen as shown in Figure 3.

⤢ *Figure 3 Splitscreen Editor with Side-by-Side Programs*

Programs are opened in the ABAP Editor with limited functionality. Additionally, the following compare functions are available on the toolbar:

► COMPARISON ON

► NEXT DIFFERENCE FROM CURSOR

► PREVIOUS DIFFERENCE FROM CURSOR

► NEXT IDENTICAL SECTION FROM CURSOR

► PREVIOUS IDENTICAL SECTION FROM CURSOR

When you click the COMPARISON ON button on the toolbar, you see whether two programs are identical or not. The lines that are not identical are flagged with a red not-equal sign. Other buttons helps you navigate through the identical or different lines on the source code.

Tip 20

Viewing and Modifying Two Parts of the Same Code at Once

You can use a tool called Split View to view and modify two different parts of the code at the same time.

While you're editing an ABAP program, you may want to open two different parts of the source code at the same time; you can use one part as a reference to change the other part, or you can change two different parts of the code at the same time. In this tip, we'll show you how to use the Split View functionality in the ABAP Editor to fulfill these requirements.

✅ And Here's How ...

Enter a specific ABAP program. To duplicate the entire code, click the split bar on the top-right corner of the ABAP Editor, and drag it down to split the editor into two parts as shown in Figure 1.

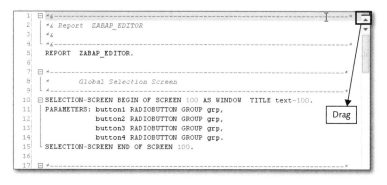

« Figure 1
Opening Split View

After you drag the bar down, the result will be as shown in Figure 2.

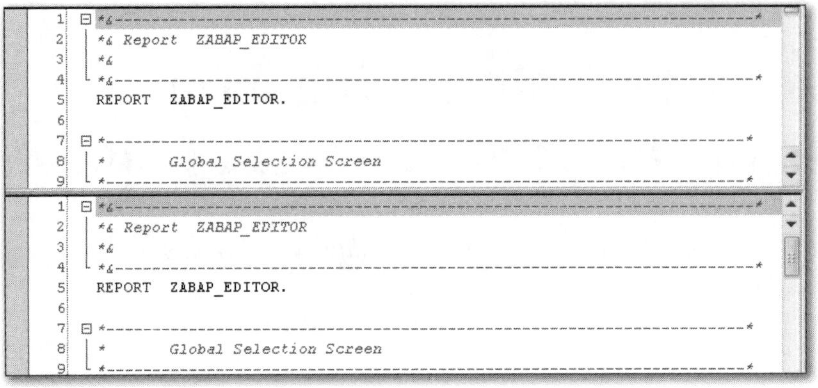

Figure 2 *Split View in the ABAP Editor*

The ABAP Editor is split into two parts. You can now navigate within the source and use any of the editors to make your changes. If you make a change in the source code in one view, it is automatically reflected in the other view.

You can use this feature for various purposes. For example, you may want to declare a new variable while programming, but you don't want to navigate away from the current position. You can split the view and use the new editor part to add your data declaration and close the split view by dragging the bar to the top of the editor after you finish.

Tip 21

Using Interactive Code Templates for Frequently Used Code Blocks

You can use predefined code templates to reduce the amount of time needed to write frequently used code blocks, or you can create your own code templates.

It's very frustrating for a developer to write the same code blocks over and over again. To solve this problem, the ABAP Editor has a code template feature that allows you to use predefined templates or to create your own interactive templates. You can also create code templates to surround any source code with a template. In this tip, we'll show you how to use this feature to reduce the amount of time to write frequently used code blocks or surround a source code with comments.

✓ And Here's How ...

While you're editing a source code in the ABAP Editor, the code template feature is active by default. You can create your own code templates or use the predefined ones for the following keywords:

- case
- define
- do
- if
- loop
- region
- try
- while

When you write any of these keywords, you'll see a special symbol that indicates that there's a code template for this keyword, as shown in Figure 1.

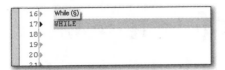

《 *Figure 1* Symbol That Indicates a Code Template Exists

When you see this symbol, press Ctrl + Enter or the Tab key to insert the code template. The template is then automatically written on the current position. For example, the following code template is inserted for keyword `case`:

```
CASE .
  WHEN .
  WHEN .
  WHEN OTHERS.
ENDCASE.
```

There are also predefined templates for following two comment blocks:

```
*********************************************************
*-------------------------------------------------------*
```

The first one is activated with *** and the second one is activated with *--. You can use these templates for creating comment entries.

You can see the whole list of templates by clicking the OPTIONS icon on the bottom-right corner of the ABAP Editor. The OPTIONS window is displayed as shown in Figure 2.

Select the CODE TEMPLATES option from the list of options to view the templates.

You can also add your own templates in this window. Click the ADD button, and a popup window opens, asking you the name and description for the template. After providing this, type your template details in the CODE text box.

You can also insert tags and variables into your templates using the INSERT TAG button. Clicking this button opens a menu with the following options:

▶ CURSORPOSITION
  After you insert the template, the cursor will be positioned on this tag.

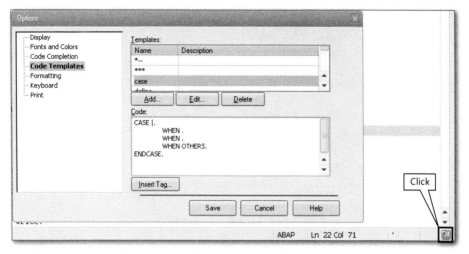

⌃ *Figure 2* *Opening the Options Window to View/Modify Code Templates*

▶ DATETIME
This tag allows you to insert the current date and time with the template.

▶ CLIPBOARD
This tag allows you to insert the clipboard content with the template.

▶ SURROUNDEDTEXT
This tag allows you to surround a text with a template in the ABAP Editor. When you select a text in the ABAP Editor and apply a template with the SURROUND-EDTEXT tag, the template content before the `SurroundedText` tag is appended before the selected text, and the rest of the template is appended after the selected text. This type of template can only be inserted by right-clicking after selecting the relevant text, and choosing FORMAT • SURROUND BY TEMPLATE.

▶ DOCUMENTNAME
This tag allows you to insert the name of the program with the template.

▶ INTERACTIVE
This tag allows you to use variables with the template. You can put the variable name between the % characters. When you insert a template with a variable, a popup window opens and asks you for the variable value as shown in Figure 3.

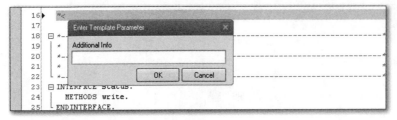

⌃ *Figure 3* *Using Variables with Templates*

For example, you can create the following template to surround a code block with your name, date, time, and an additional comment:

```
"<YOUR NAME %DateTime%>
"%Additional Info%
%SurroundedText%
"</YOUR NAME %DateTime%>
```

You can use this template if you make a change in an ABAP program and want to insert a comment about your change. Select the change you made, and apply the template by selecting FORMAT • SURROUND BY TEMPLATE.

After you apply this template, your change is surrounded with your comment. You can change the template content according to your commenting style.

Tip **22**

Using Enhanced Copy and Paste Functionalities

You can use enhanced copy and paste functionalities to use the ABAP Editor more effectively.

The copy and paste functionality is one of the most useful features that developers use in software development processes. It makes life easier by not having to type the same things multiple times. Consequently, the ABAP Editor has improved copy and paste capabilities that allow you to store multiple items in the clipboard and paste by selecting from a list of these items.

✅ And Here's How ...

The ABAP Editor provides the clipboard ring and buffers for enhanced copy and paste functionality. Let's explore both of these in the following subsections.

Clipboard Ring

The clipboard ring adds an extra functionality to the normal copy/paste function by allowing you to store your last 12 clipboard items in historical sequence. You don't need to do anything special to enable this functionality. When you use the normal copy function (Ctrl + C), the clipboard content is also stored in the clipboard ring. You can access the clipboard ring by pressing the Ctrl + Shift + V key sequence or by selecting MORE • EXTENDED PASTE from the context menu. The clipboard content up to the last 12 items is displayed in the list as shown in Figure 1, and you can select any of the items to insert into the code.

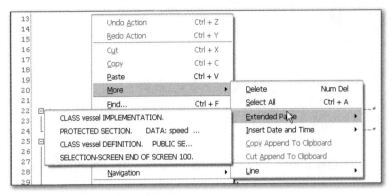

⌃ *Figure 1* Extended Paste Menu

Note that the EXTENDED PASTE menu is active only when you have used the copy function at least twice. The content of the clipboard ring is available only for the current session, and is cleared when you exit from the ABAP Editor.

If you select a text and use the function COPY APPEND TO CLIPBOARD in the same menu, the selected text is appended to the last clipboard item. The CUT APPEND TO CLIPBOARD function also does the same function but cuts the selected text from the ABAP Editor.

Buffers

The ABAP Editor has three separate buffers—X Buffer, Y Buffer, and Z Buffer that you can use like a clipboard. These buffers can be used to copy and paste between sessions in the same SAP system. You can access the buffers by selecting BLOCK/ BUFFER from the context menu or by choosing UTILITIES • BLOCK/BUFFER.

The following functions are available in the BLOCK/BUFFER menu:

▶ COPY TO X/Y/Z BUFFER

▶ INSERT X/Y/Z BUFFER

▶ EDIT BUFFER

You can add a text to a buffer by selecting the text in the ABAP Editor and using the COPY TO X/Y/Z BUFFER function. Later, you can use the INSERT X/Y/Z BUFFER function to insert the buffer content into the editor. You can also edit buffers with the EDIT BUFFER function.

Searching in Real Time with Incremental Search

The incremental search feature can be used to search a text in the ABAP Editor as you type.

Most developers are familiar with the classical search function in the ABAP Editor—enter the search term into the search dialog, and the system searches for that term in the source code. On the other hand, the ABAP Editor's other search function—incremental search—allows you to enter the search term character by character while the cursor jumps to the first match for that character combination as you type. You can perform real-time searches by changing the search term according to the results while you type.

✅ And Here's How ...

You can turn on incremental search by right-clicking on the ABAP Editor and selecting the FIND INCREMENTAL function or pressing the shortcut ⌃Ctrl + ⌃I. The mouse pointer icon changes to binoculars with a downward-pointing arrow as shown in Figure 1, indicating that you can start searching.

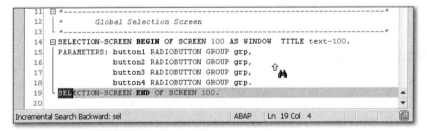

```
11  ⊟ *----------------------------------------------------------------
12  |  *          Global Selection Screen
13  L *----------------------------------------------------------------
14  ⊟ SELECTION-SCREEN BEGIN OF SCREEN 100 AS WINDOW   TITLE text-100.
15  | PARAMETERS: button1 RADIOBUTTON GROUP grp,
16  |             button2 RADIOBUTTON GROUP grp,              🔍
17  |             button3 RADIOBUTTON GROUP grp,              ⇩
18  |             button4 RADIOBUTTON GROUP grp.
19  L SELECTION-SCREEN END OF SCREEN 100.
20
21
22  ⊟ *----------------------------------------------------------------
```

Incremental Search: sel | ABAP | Ln 19 Col 4

⚠ *Figure 1* Incremental Search Forward

There is no popup window to type in the search term. Just start typing and the cursor automatically moves to the first instance of the search term. Press Ctrl + I anytime to jump to the next match in the source code. The incremental search can be cancelled anytime by pressing Esc or any of the arrow keys during the search.

Incremental search is performed forward by default. If you want to search backward, select MORE • FIND INCREMENTAL PREVIOUS in the context menu, or use the shortcut Ctrl + Shift + I.

This time, the upward arrow appears on the binoculars icon as shown in Figure 2, and the search is performed backwards from the current position.

```
11  ⊟ *--------------------------------------------------------------*
12  |  *          Global Selection Screen
13  L *--------------------------------------------------------------*
14  ⊟ SELECTION-SCREEN BEGIN OF SCREEN 100 AS WINDOW   TITLE text-100.
15  | PARAMETERS: button1 RADIOBUTTON GROUP grp,
16  |             button2 RADIOBUTTON GROUP grp,
17  |             button3 RADIOBUTTON GROUP grp,       ⇧🔍
18  |             button4 RADIOBUTTON GROUP grp.
19  L SELECTION-SCREEN END OF SCREEN 100.
20
```

Incremental Search Backward: sel | ABAP | Ln 19 Col 4

⚠ *Figure 2* Incremental Search Backward

Using incremental search instead of normal search saves you time, especially when you want to jump quickly to another part of the source code or are trying to find the instances of a keyword.

Using Improved Navigation Features in the ABAP Editor

You can navigate through long and complex source code faster by using specific navigation tools in the ABAP Editor.

While developing ABAP programs, you usually need to navigate through the ABAP Editor window to access different parts of the source code. You can use scrolling tools for small programs, but when you develop complex programs, you might need additional features and shortcuts such as creating bookmarks or jumping to the specific positions of the source code quickly. In this tip, we'll show you simple but powerful tricks to enrich your navigation experience as you use the ABAP Editor.

And Here's How ...

You can use the following navigation tools in the ABAP Editor to navigate through the source code faster.

Go to Line

If you know the line number of the specific code, you can navigate directly to that line by using this function. To access this function, right-click in the ABAP Editor and select GO TO LINE from the NAVIGATION menu, or press $\boxed{\text{Ctrl}}$ + $\boxed{0}$. A popup window opens and asks you for the line number you want to jump to, as shown in Figure 1.

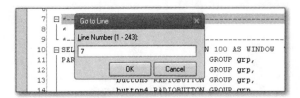

« Figure 1 *Jump to the Line Number Using the Go to Line Function*

The cursor will be positioned to the line number provided after you click OK. You can't enter a number that is larger than the total lines of the source code. The maximum value that you can enter is also shown on the popup window. If you enter a number larger than the maximum value, it's automatically changed to the maximum value.

Go to Last Change
When you navigate through the source code after making changes in different places, you can go back to the position of your last change by using this function. Right-click in the ABAP Editor and select GO TO LAST CHANGE from the NAVIGATION menu. This will take you to the last line you modified. If you save and activate the program, the history of your changes is reset, and you can't access your last changed line with this function anymore.

Bookmarks
You can create bookmarks for the lines in the source code to go back to these positions easily. You have an option to create up to 10 numbered bookmarks and an unlimited number of additional bookmarks. You can access the BOOKMARKS menu by right-clicking on the left margin of the ABAP Editor as shown in Figure 2.

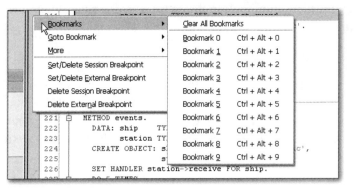

« Figure 2 Bookmarks Menu

Numbered bookmarks are used to assign a specific number to a bookmark. You can access it from the BOOKMARKS menu in the context menu of the left margin and choose a number from 0 to 9 to assign to a bookmark. You can also assign a numbered bookmark to a current line position directly from the editor by pressing Ctrl + Alt and the number of your choice. The lines with bookmarks are shown with a numbered flag in the left margin. Later, you can navigate to these bookmarks by selecting the appropriate number from the GOTO BOOKMARK group in the context menu of the left margin as shown in Figure 3 or by using the shortcut Ctrl and the number key.

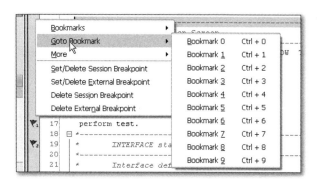

« Figure 3 Go to Bookmark

The BOOKMARKS menu works in toggle mode. If you select the bookmark menu for the lines with a bookmark, the current bookmark will be removed.

Unnumbered bookmarks are used to assign a bookmark without a number to a line. You can assign an unnumbered bookmark by selecting TOGGLE BOOKMARK from the MORE menu in the context menu of the left margin or by pressing Ctrl + Alt + M. It will add an unnumbered bookmark if a bookmark doesn't already exist and delete the bookmark if there is already a bookmark on the line. You can use NEXT BOOKMARK (Ctrl + M) and PREVIOUS BOOKMARK (Ctrl + Shift + M) from the same menu to navigate through the bookmarks in the source code.

These simple but powerful navigation features help you move through the source code more efficiently during the development process of ABAP programs. You can develop your programs without using any of these tools, but you will quickly recognize the benefits of using these navigation features after you start using them.

Creating Custom Statement Patterns

You can create templates for frequently used code patterns to reuse them later by inserting them into the ABAP programs.

Several types of statement patterns can be inserted by the pattern function in the ABAP Editor. The pattern function helps you insert complex statements into the programs instead of writing them manually. You can also create your own templates for frequently used code patterns.

✔ And Here's How ...

You can insert statement patterns in the ABAP Editor by using the PATTERN function on the toolbar. A popup window shows the statement types that you can choose from as shown in Figure 1.

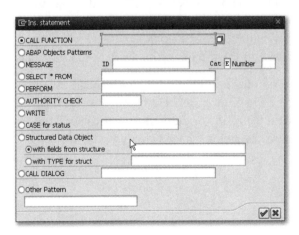

« Figure 1 *Insert Statement Window*

Choose one of the statement types and provide the relevant details. Then the source code template for the selected statement will be inserted into the source code. For example, if you select CALL FUNCTION and enter "BAPI_FLIGHT_ CHECKAVAILABILITY" in the input field next to the radio button, the following source code will be inserted into the ABAP Editor:

```
CALL FUNCTION 'BAPI_FLIGHT_CHECKAVAILABILITY'
   EXPORTING
      airlineid          =
      connectionid       =
      flightdate         =
*  IMPORTING
*     AVAILABILITY       =
*  TABLES
*     RETURN             =
          .
```

You can then add the missing fields into the code. This feature is great because you don't have to remember the detailed syntax for the statements.

Notice that there is also an OTHER PATTERN radio button at the bottom of the popup dialog. You can create your own patterns and use this option to insert the custom pattern into the code. While you're in the ABAP Editor, select the following menu path to start creating your own pattern:

UTILITIES • MORE UTILITIES • EDIT PATTERN • CREATE PATTERN

In the CREATE PATTERN popup that opens, enter the name of the pattern and click OK. A text editor opens to allow you to create the template as shown in Figure 2.

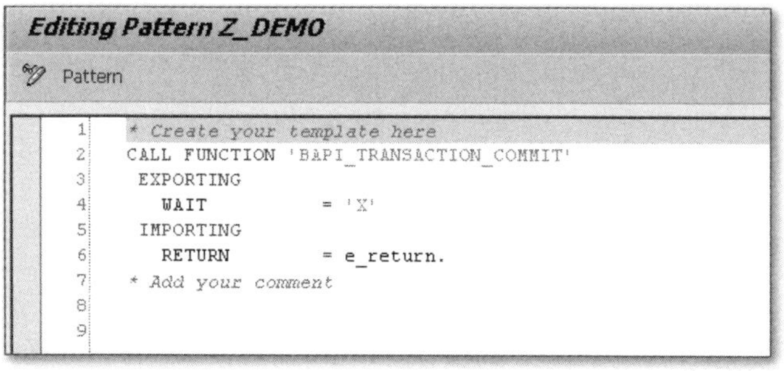

《 Figure 2 *Create a Custom Pattern*

Any ABAP statement or comment lines can be used in the pattern. You can create patterns with up to 100 lines. When you save the pattern, it will be available in the OTHER PATTERN option of the INS. STATEMENT dialog. Later, you can display, change, or delete existing patterns in the same CREATE PATTERN menu group.

Formatting Source Code with Pretty Printer

You can use the Pretty Printer tool in the ABAP Editor to format source code and make it easier to read, analyze, and modify.

Have you ever found yourself in a situation where you have to debug or modify a source code, but it's impossible to read? Every programmer wants to work on readable and nicely formatted source code. This is particularly important if you are analyzing or modifying the code written by someone else. In this tip, we'll show you how to use the Pretty Printer tool in the ABAP Editor to transform the source code into a more readable format.

And Here's How ...

You can execute the Pretty Printer tool by using the PRETTY PRINTER button on the toolbar while you are in the ABAP Editor. It standardizes the source code by formatting the layout conforming to the ABAP layout standards recommended by SAP. This ensures that every developer is writing ABAP programs in similar formats.

When you run the Pretty Printer tool, the following actions are performed on the source code:

- Automatically generates comment blocks for some statements, such as subroutines, to provide you a template for building comments.
- Indents your source code to improve the readability.
- Places the following keywords at the beginning of a separate line:
  - Event blocks: `INITIALIZATION`, `AT SELECTION-SCREEN`, `START-OF-SELECTION`, `GET`, `END-OF-SELETION`

▶ Form statements

▶ Module statements

▶ Places control (IF, WHILE, CASE) and INCLUDE keywords on a separate line and indents them according to the indentation rules.

▶ Precedes event keywords by a blank line or a comment line.

▶ Indents all command lines and control structures by two columns.

You can adjust Pretty Printer settings via UTILITIES • SETTINGS. Figure 1 shows the settings window.

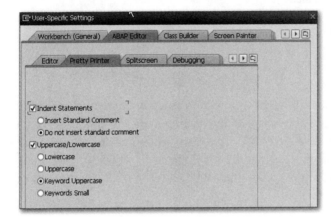

《 Figure 1 *Pretty Printer Settings*

You can adjust the following options in this window:

▶ INDENT STATEMENTS
Select this if you want to indent the code according to the guidelines described previously. You can also select the option to insert the standard comments with Pretty Printer.

▶ UPPERCASE/LOWERCASE
Select this to standardize the display of the source code. You can select one of the following options if you want to perform case conversion:

▶ LOWERCASE: All source code is converted to lowercase.

▶ UPPERCASE: All source code is converted to uppercase.

▶ KEYWORD UPPERCASE: Keywords are converted to uppercase, and the rest is converted to lowercase.

▶ KEYWORDS SMALL: Keywords are converted to lowercase, and the rest is converted to uppercase.

Tip 27

Using Code Hints as Prompts When Writing Code

You can prompt possible keywords and identifiers by using the Code Hints feature, and thus avoid confusing programming languages or confusing keywords.

Every programming language has its own syntax and language-specific keywords. When you use more than one programming language, it's very common to confuse the keywords and syntax and make a syntax error in the source code. The Code Hints feature that exists in the ABAP Editor helps you write code quickly and without mistakes by suggesting possible keywords and identifiers while you type. In this tip, we'll show you how you can set up and use the Code Hints feature while using the ABAP Editor.

✓ And Here's How ...

The Code Hints feature allows you to write code without the need to remember the full syntax of the keyword. The system displays the possible keywords and identifiers as you type characters in the ABAP Editor. Another advantage of this feature is that it shows you the keywords that you don't know and helps improve your ABAP knowledge.

Code hints are shown in a tooltip as you type. If there is only one option available, it's displayed in black letters on a yellow background as shown in Figure 1.

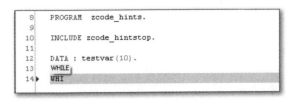

« Figure 1 *Code Hint When Only One Option Is Available*

If more than one option is available, the most relevant one is displayed in white letters on a black background as shown in Figure 2.

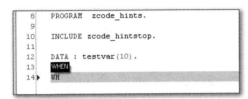

« Figure 2 *Code Hint When More Than One Option Is Available*

When a code hint is displayed, press [Tab] to insert the suggested keyword into the code.

To adjust the settings for the Code Hints feature, open the CODE COMPLETION SETTINGS window by clicking the icon at the bottom-right of the editor and selecting CODE COMPLETION from the list of options. Figure 3 shows the settings that can be configured in this window.

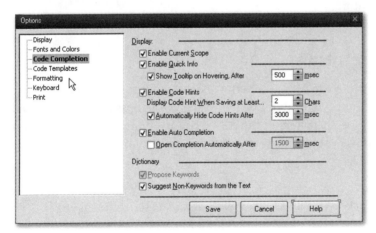

« Figure 3 *Code Hints Settings*

You can enable the following settings:

► The ENABLE CODE HINTS checkbox allows you to see the code hints in the editor.

► The DISPLAY CODE HINT WHEN SAVING AT LEAST field allows you to set the number of characters that you should type to see code hints.

► The AUTOMATICALLY HIDE CODE HINTS AFTER field allows you to set the amount of time that the code hint should be displayed. After that amount of time, the code hint disappears.

► The SUGGEST NON-KEYWORDS FROM THE TEXT field allows you to enable and disable the suggestion of identifier hints. Identifiers are also suggested with the keywords if you select this option.

Tip 28

Using Code Completion to Complete Statements

You can write code faster by using the Code Completion feature to see the list of possible keywords and identifiers for the current source code position.

When you're writing an ABAP program, you usually need to use several programming entities such as function modules, classes, subroutines, and variables. You may not always remember the name of these programming entities when you need to use them, even if you know the syntax of the ABAP language very well. The Code Completion feature in the ABAP Editor helps you write your code much faster by listing your possible statements for the current source code position.

✓ And Here's How ...

When you're writing an ABAP program, start the Code Completion feature by pressing Ctrl + Space after you write a few letters. The system will display a list of possible programming entities that you can insert to the current cursor position. The following programming entities can be inserted by the Code Completion tool:

▸ Types and variables

▸ Function modules, classes, and interfaces

▸ Implemented interfaces and Business Add-Ins (BAdIs)

▸ Subroutines

▸ Parameters of function modules, classes, and subroutines

▸ Keywords

Unlike the Code Hints tool discussed in Tip 27, the Code Completion tools runs on the server side and brings only the syntactically correct list to the user. All possible options are listed in a dropdown box that you can easily select and insert into the code as shown in Figure 1.

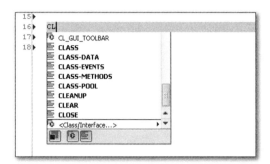

《 Figure 1 *Sample Code Completion List*

Several types or entities are shown in the same list as you can see in Figure 1. You can even open a Class/Interface search dialog by selecting the <CLASS/INTER-FACE…> option at the end of the list. If you were inserting a function module, you would see <FUNCTION MODULE…> instead of <CLASS/INTERFACE…>.

The items that exactly match the current cursor position are displayed in bold. Other items need additional entities to be inserted. For example, in Figure 1, all of the keywords are displayed in bold except the class CL_GUI_TOOLBAR because you need to insert a method name after inserting the class name in the editor. You can filter and show only the bold items by clicking the BOLD button at the bottom of the list.

Each type of entity is displayed with a different icon, and you can filter the list by clicking the relevant icon at the bottom of the list as shown in Figure 2.

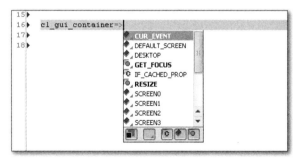

《 Figure 2 *Code Completion List with Different Types of Entities and Filter Buttons*

There are also additional filter buttons that allow you to filter by other attributes such as visibility, type, and so on.

Adjust the Code Completion settings according to your needs by clicking the icon at the bottom-right of the editor and selecting CODE COMPLETION from the list of options. Figure 3 shows the options that you can adjust.

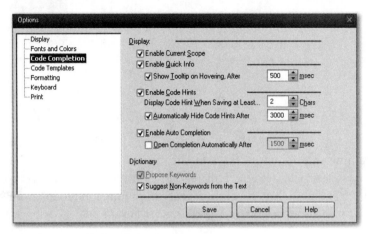

⌃ *Figure 3* *Code Completion Options*

You can adjust the following settings:

▶ The ENABLE CURRENT SCOPE option allows you to show the number of entities and groups shown in the CODE COMPLETION list. The scope information is displayed on the left side of the status bar.

▶ The ENABLE QUICK INFO option enables the quick info box when you position your cursor over a block as shown in Figure 4.

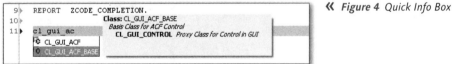

≪ *Figure 4* *Quick Info Box*

▶ The ENABLE AUTO COMPLETION option enables the code completion for the entities of classes after you insert =>.

▶ The OPEN COMPLETION AUTOMATICALLY AFTER option allows you to set the amount of time in milliseconds that the system waits to open the dropdown list.

Part 3

Function Builder

Things You'll Learn in this Section

The Function Builder is one of the major tools of the ABAP Workbench, allowing developers to break programs into reusable modules. It's also the central tool that developers use to create, modify, and test function groups and function modules. You can create custom function modules using the Function Builder in addition to the many predefined function modules provided by SAP.

You can also use the RFC interface to call function modules from the remote SAP systems. Function modules are used extensively in SAP, which requires ABAP developers to use the Function Builder often. In this part of the book, we'll show you practical ways of testing function modules and using the RFC interface to call function modules between SAP systems.

Saving Test Data for Function Modules

You can save time by saving the test data for a function module and using the same data to test it again later.

The Function Builder has a test interface that allows you to fill the importing parameters, structures, and tables, and then run the function module with these values. You'll sometimes find that you need to test the same function module with the same parameters several times. However, it can be frustrating and difficult to fill in the same parameters again and again if the function module has a complex interface. In this tip, we'll show you how to save the test parameters for later use to eliminate the problem.

✓ And Here's How ...

Run the test tool for a function module in the Function Builder using the TEST button (▦) to open a parameter screen that allows you to fill in the test parameters. You can fill in test data for all types of import parameters: normal parameters, structures, and tables. When you're finished filling in all of the necessary parameters, save them by clicking SAVE on the toolbar for later use. A popup window opens as shown in Figure 1 to let you enter a description for the test data in the COMMENTS field.

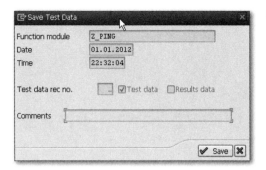

《 *Figure 1* Save Test Data Popup

Click SAVE to finish the process. You can now access all saved test data of a function module by clicking the TEST DATA DIRECTORY button on the toolbar. As shown in Figure 2, all records in the Test Data Directory are listed, and you can double-click any of these records to transfer test data to the function module interface you're working with.

Data record number	Date	Time	Short text	S
1	01.01.2012	22:29:53	Date Problem	
2	01.01.2012	22:31:38	Date Problem - New Test Data	
3	01.01.2012	22:31:51	Test New Parameter	
4	01.01.2012	22:37:08	Another Test	

Test Data Directory: Single Tests

Regression test   Show test result

☆ *Figure 2* Test Data Directory

You can also select test data by positioning the cursor on the record and pressing F2 or by choosing EDIT • GET TEST DATA.

When you're finished testing with the test data, you can delete any record to keep the list clean by positioning the cursor on the record and clicking the DELETE button on the toolbar.

Running Function Modules Successively with Test Sequences

You can use test sequences to test more than one function module in the same logical unit of work.

The Function Builder has an interface that allows you to test function modules; you provide test parameters within the test interface and then see the results on the screen. Some function modules are required to run one after another in the same context. However, you can't run them one by one using the classical test methods because some functions in the sequence might depend on the previous one, and the database must be committed only if all functions in the sequence run successfully. For this purpose, you can use test sequences to run function modules sequentially.

✅ And Here's How ...

The main difference with using test sequences instead of the normal test process is that all function modules are run in the same context. Using text sequences are especially important for Business Application Programming Interfaces (BAPIs). When you run a BAPI, you must call function module `BAPI_TRANSACTION_COMMIT` to commit the changes into the database. Otherwise, the results are not saved into the database. However, when you run `BAPI_TRANSACTION_COMMIT` normally after the original BAPI, it runs in a different context and doesn't commit the changes of the BAPI. You can run these two function modules in the test sequence, which runs the function modules in the same context and produces the desired result.

Use the following menu path to start test sequences in the Function Builder while you're editing a function module:

FUNCTION MODULE • TEST • TEST SEQUENCES

A popup window opens as shown in Figure 1, where you list the function modules that you want to test.

« *Figure 1 Select Function Modules to Run in Test Sequence*

Click the EXECUTE button () on the popup, and a test screen opens where you fill in the test parameters for the first function module. This is the same window that you use to the test a single function module. Click EXECUTE to run the function module, and the results are displayed.

Click BACK, and the test screen opens for the second function module that you input in the ENTER TEST SEQUENCES list. The same process continues until the last function module.

After you finish testing the last function module in the list, the system asks you to save the test sequence to let you use the same sequence later. You can access the saved test sequences with the GET SEQUENCE button on the popup window where you listed the function modules (see Figure 1). The saved test sequences are displayed in a list as shown in Figure 2.

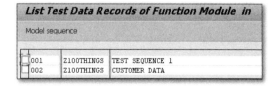

« *Figure 2 Saved List of Test Sequences*

You can open a test sequence by double-clicking or selecting it from the list and clicking MODEL SEQUENCE on the toolbar.

101

Creating and Using Remote-Enabled Function Modules

You can use RFC destinations to call function modules on remote SAP systems as if they're in your local system.

One of the great features of function modules is that they can be called remotely from other systems if their type is remote-enabled. This feature helps you when you want to retrieve data from another SAP system. In this tip, you'll learn how to use the Function Builder to create remote-enabled function modules on the remote system and call this function module from your local system using the remote function call (RFC) interface.

 And Here's How ...

When you want to call a function module from another system, you first have to define this system in RFC destinations using Transaction SM59 or using the following menu path:

TOOLS • ADMINISTRATION • ADMINISTRATION • NETWORK • RFC DESTINATIONS

Use the following procedure to create an RFC destination:

1. Go to Transaction SM59.
2. Click the CREATE button on the toolbar.
3. Enter the name of the destination in the RFC DESTINATION field.
4. Select CONNECTION TO ABAP SYSTEM in the CONNECTION TYPE field.

5. Enter the description in the DESCRIPTION fields.

6. Fill in the system details in the TECHNICAL SETTINGS tab.

7. Fill in the logon information in the LOGON & SECURITY tab.

Your screen should now look like Figure 1.

⟰ *Figure 1* *Creating an RFC Destination for the ABAP System*

You can test the connection with the CONNECTION TEST button on the toolbar.

When you successfully create the RFC destination, you can call function modules from this system in ABAP programs by adding the DESTINATION clause to the CALL FUNCTION statement as shown in the following example:

```
CALL FUNCTION 'Z_PING'
  DESTINATION 'A73CLNT001'
  EXPORTING
    i_name          = lv_name
  IMPORTING
    e_message       = lv_message.
```

Note that the processing type of a function module you're calling remotely must be selected as REMOTE-ENABLED MODULE as shown in Figure 2.

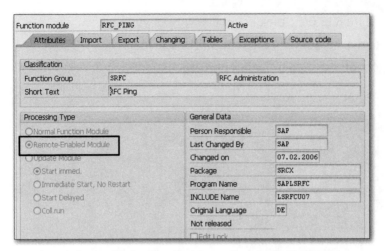

⊼ *Figure 2 Setting the Function Module as a Remote-Enabled Module*

Using Predefined RFC Destination BACK to Call Function Modules

In RFC functions, you can call back the caller system using the predefined RFC destination instead of creating a new one.

When you call a function module from a remote system using an RFC interface, you may need to call back a function module of the remote function's calling system. Because there's already an active RFC connection between the two systems, you can avoid the process of manually creating and maintaining an RFC destination in the remote system and use the existing connection to call RFC functions from the caller system instead. In this tip, we'll show you how to call function modules on the calling system using the predefined RFC destination BACK.

And Here's How ...

By using the predefined RFC destination BACK in the SAP system, you don't have to create it manually as an RFC destination in Transaction SM59. This RFC destination can only be used in remote-enabled functions and automatically links to the system that remotely calls this function module.

Figure 1 shows an example scenario using RFC destination BACK. Here, there is only one RFC destination defined in the local system to call Function Module Z_TEST on the remote system. There is no need to create an RFC destination on the remote system to call Function Module Z_TEST2. RFC destination BACK can be used for this purpose.

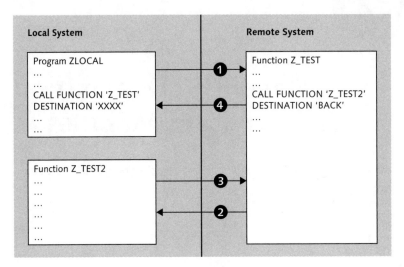

⌃ **Figure 1** *Example Scenario using RFC Destination BACK*

You can only use RFC destination BACK in the function module that is called synchronously. However, you can use all types of RFCs when you call back a function module from the calling system.

Note that if you use the RFC destination BACK in a function module that is called locally, the system produces a short dump.

Part 4

Class Builder

Things You'll Learn in this Section

The object-oriented (OO) programming model, as compared to structured programming, allows you to build and manage more complex and robust applications. This involves building your programs around objects instead of trying to build complete logic into a single program. This method allows you to separate complex programs into smaller units, which makes it easier to develop in a team, analyze, and debug. As OO programming becomes more popular, it's important to adapt your ABAP programs to new programming concepts.

In this part of the book, you'll learn tips and tricks about the Class Builder, which allows you to use OO programming techniques in the ABAP Workbench.

Maintaining Classes with the Source Code-Based Class Builder[1]

You can edit the source of global classes in a single editor window instead of using form-based screens.

The Class Builder has an interface that allows you to maintain global classes using form-based screens. When you modify the class definition in a form-based screen, the source code is automatically generated, and you don't need to worry about the detailed syntax of the class definition. Sometimes, you may need to see the complete source code of the class and modify it directly within the source code instead of form-based screens. You can use the source code-based Class Builder for this purpose.

✓ And Here's How ...

You can switch between the source code-based and form-based class Builder screens on the main screen of the Class Builder. When you open the global class in the Class Builder using Transaction SE24 or Transaction SE80, the form-based Class Builder opens by default as shown in Figure 1.

---

1 Applicable to SAP NetWeaver release 7.3 and later.

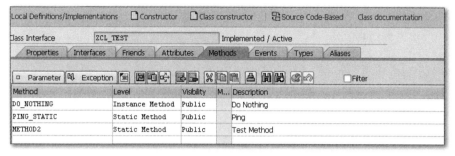

⩘ *Figure 1* Form-Based Class Builder

You can switch to the source code-based Class Builder by clicking the SOURCE
CODE-BASED button on the toolbar. Now you can see the complete class source
code as shown in Figure 2 and modify the class source code directly.

```
ttern   Pretty Printer   ⚡   🗈 Local Definitions/Implementations    🗗 Form-Based    Interface Documentation

Class Source              Active (Revised)

    1  ⊟ CLASS zcl_test DEFINITION
    2      PUBLIC
    3      FINAL
    4      CREATE PUBLIC .
    5
    6    PUBLIC SECTION.
    7  ⊟ *"* public components of class ZCL_TEST
    8  ├ *"* do not include other source files here!!!
    9
   10      METHODS do_nothing
   11        IMPORTING
   12          !p1 TYPE string
   13          !p2 TYPE string OPTIONAL
   14        RETURNING
   15          value(r1) TYPE string .
   16      CLASS-METHODS ping_static .
   17      CLASS-METHODS method2 .
```

⩘ *Figure 2* Source Code-Based Class Builder

Set the default view of the Class Builder to the source code-based Class Builder in
the CLASS BUILDER tab of the USER-SPECIFIC SETTINGS window. Open this window
by clicking UTILITIES • SETTINGS. Select the SOURCE CODE-BASED CLASS BUILDER
checkbox as shown in Figure 3.

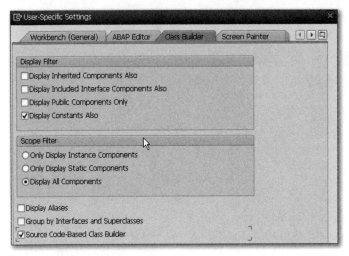

⏫ *Figure 3 Switching the Default View to Source Code-Based Class Builder*

Now, the source code-based view is opened by default when you open the class in the Class Builder. You can still switch to form-based view using the FORM-BASED button on the toolbar.

You can navigate to class attributes, methods, events, and method implementations using the CLASS/INTERFACE NAVIGATOR tool which you open by pressing Ctrl + F5. Figure 4 displays the CLASS/INTERFACE NAVIGATOR window where you can also filter out all entities using the FILTER field.

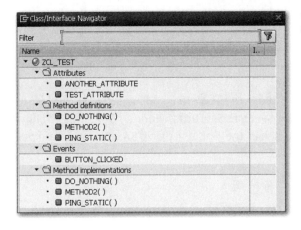

《 *Figure 4 Class/Interface Navigator*

Note that you can only use the source code-based Class Builder for standard classes. Persistent classes, exception classes, and global test classes aren't supported.

Renaming Methods of Classes Consistently with the Refactoring Assistant

You can use the Refactoring Assistant to find all instances of local and global methods of the classes and rename them consistently.

When you want to rename a method of a global class, you have to take into consideration all of the method calls pointing to this method to prevent possible errors due to the renaming. All local methods and global programs calling this method must be updated with the new method name. Instead of guessing and searching all of the places where the name may appear, you can use the Refactoring Assistant to rename the method consistently in all places it's used.

And Here's How ...

The Refactoring Assistant can be used for classes only in the source code-based Class Builder. You can switch to the source code-based Class Builder using the SOURCE CODE-BASED button on the toolbar when you open the global class in the Class Builder.

First, open the source code of the class in the Class Builder using Transaction SE24 to start the refactoring process. Then, position the cursor on the method definition that you want to rename, and start the Refactoring Assistant by choosing REFACTORING • RENAME as shown in Figure 1.

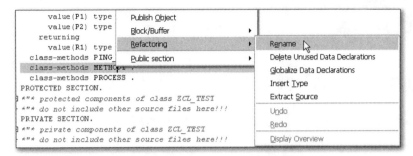

```
    value(P1) type    Publish Object
    value(P2) type    Block/Buffer              ▶
  returning
    value(R1) type    Refactoring               ▶    Rename
  class-methods PING_   Public section          ▶    Delete Unused Data Declarations
  class-methods METHOD1 .                             Globalize Data Declarations
  class-methods PROCESS .
PROTECTED SECTION.                                    Insert Type
*"* protected components of class ZCL_TEST            Extract Source
*"* do not include other source files here!!!         Undo
PRIVATE SECTION.
*"* private components of class ZCL_TEST              Redo
*"* do not include other source files here!!!        Display Overview
```

⌄ Figure 1 *Starting the Refactoring Assistant to Rename a Method*

The refactoring wizard opens, and you can step through the wizard using the CON-TINUE button. Type the new name for the method in the second step as shown in Figure 2, and click the CONTINUE button.

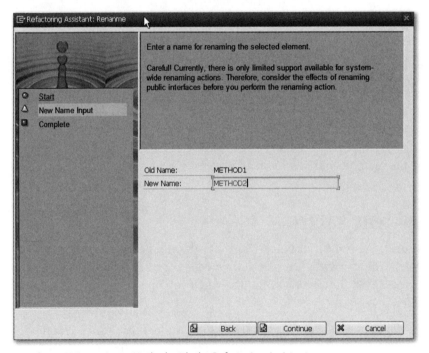

⌄ Figure 2 *Renaming a Method with the Refactoring Assistant*

Now the method name is updated in the source code and also in all programs that use it after you finish the wizard.

You can open the preview screen to see the list of changed objects by right-clicking at any place in the editor and selecting REFACTORING • DISPLAY OVERVIEW from the context menu.

The preview window appears (see Figure 3), and you can navigate through the list to see the changes in the objects.

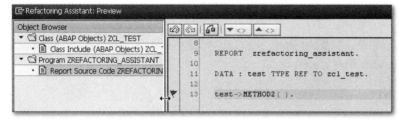

⌃ *Figure 3* *Preview the Changes*

Using Persistent Classes to Access Database Tables

You can create persistent classes using the Class Builder tool to adopt an OO approach to the programs that have database accesses.

In traditional programming, data access is performed using SQL statements. However, in an OO programming model, data access is typically implemented using objects. In this tip, we'll show you how to use the Class Builder tools to create persistent classes in the ABAP Workbench to access data in an OO way.

✅ And Here's How ...

The process of creating persistent classes is different from creating usual ABAP classes. When you start creating a class in the Class Builder using Transaction SE24 (or in Object Navigator), select the PERSISTENT CLASS radio button in the initial window, and enter the name and description of the class as shown in Figure 1.

《 Figure 1 *Selecting the Persistent Class Type*

Note that the persistent class name must start with the namespace plus the prefix
"CL_" (e.g., ZCL_ or /NAMESPACE/CL_).

After you save the class, the system generates two more classes in the background
that will help you access the persistent class. For example, if you name the persistent class ZCL_OO_PERS_SFLIGHT, base class ZCB_OO_PERS_SFLIGHT and agent class
ZCA_OO_PERS_SFLIGHT are automatically generated.

After creating the persistent class, you can start mapping the class with the database
using the PERSISTENT button on the toolbar. A popup window asks you to enter the
name of the table that you want to access. Enter the name of the table and click
the CONTINUE button. The MAPPING ASSISTANT screen opens, and you can map
the fields from the lower table TABLES/FIELDS to the upper table CLASS/ATTRIBUTE
as shown in Figure 2. You can map any field by double-clicking the field name and
then clicking the SET ATTRIBUTE VALUES button (▲) as shown in the figure.

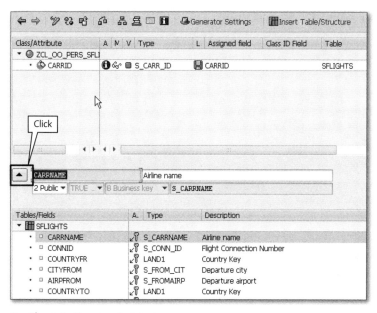

⁂ *Figure 2* *Mapping Assistant*

After you save and activate the persistent class, the get and set methods to retrieve
values of the table and write a value to the table, respectively, are generated automatically by the system. These methods are automatically generated even if you
add your own attributes to the class. You can also modify the generated get and
set methods in the Class Builder to implement your own logic.

The following sample program shows how you can use the persistent class in your ABAP programs:

```
PARAMETERS: p_carrid TYPE sflight-carrid,
            p_connid TYPE sflight-connid,
            p_fldate TYPE sflight-fldate.
DATA: flights TYPE REF TO zcl_oo_pers_sflight,
      lv_planetype TYPE sflight-planetype.
START-OF-SELECTION.
flights = zca_oo_pers_sflight->agent->get_persistent(
  i_carrid = p_carrid
  i_connid = p_connid
  i_fldate = p_fldate ).
lv_planetype = flights->get_planetype( ).
WRITE:/ 'Plane Type'(001), lv_planetype.
```

As you see in the source code, you're accessing database tables without using any SQL statements. All database operations are performed in the persistent class methods.

Managing Exceptions with Exception Classes

You can create exception classes to enhance the exception handling capabilities of your ABAP programs with custom attributes for error handling.

The OO programming model has significantly changed the way exceptions are handled in ABAP programs. As an example, it was only possible to use return codes to give information about the error in old-style exceptions. The class type exception class has been introduced to the ABAP Workbench to allow you to return additional information with the exception. In this tip, you'll learn how to create a simple exception class.

And Here's How ...

Perform the following operations to create an exception class:

1. Go to Transaction SE24.
2. Enter the name of the class and click the CREATE button. Note that you must begin the exception class name with the namespace plus "CX_" (e.g., ZCX_ or /NAMESPACE/CX_).
3. Enter a short description for the class in the DESCRIPTION field.
4. Select EXCEPTION CLASS in the CLASS TYPE group box.
5. Choose SAVE.

Now that you've created an exception class, you can add additional attributes and texts.

The ATTRIBUTES tab allows you to return additional information with the exception. You can see the default attributes that are inherited from the Superclass CX_STATIC_CHECK (the first six attributes in the ATTRIBUTES column are in blue color) as shown in Figure 1.

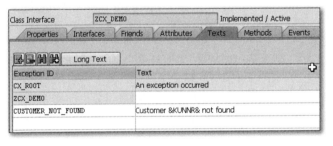

⏫ *Figure 1 Default Attributes Inherited from the Superclass*

You can also add your own attributes to return additional attributes with the exception. For example, create an attribute KUNNR with type KUNNR. We'll use this attribute in the exception texts. Make sure to select the READ-ONLY flag to prevent users from changing the attribute value.

In the TEXTS tab, you can create exception texts. A default text whose ID is the same as the class name is automatically created. You can also add additional texts. In the text part, you can refer to attribute values by enclosing the attribute name in "&" characters as shown in Figure 2.

《 *Figure 2 Creating Exception ID and Parametric Texts*

You've now created your exception class and maintained custom attributes and exception IDs. Now the ZCX_DEMO class is ready to use. You can use the following code block to raise an exception using this exception class:

```
RAISE EXCEPTION TYPE zcx_demo
    EXPORTING textid = zcx_demo=>customer_not_found
              kunnr  = '002124937'.
```

Additionally, you can catch the exception in the main program using the following code block:

```
CATCH zcx_demo INTO demo.
    text = demo->get_text( ).
    write:/ text.
```

If you hadn't used exception classes, you would only able to return an error code indicating that a CUSTOMER_NOT_FOUND exception occurred. As you can see in the example, exception classes allow you to return the customer number with the exception and produce more meaningful error messages.

Part 5

ABAP Debugger

Things You'll Learn in this Section

Debuggers allow developers to locate and fix any bugs or problems that exist in the source code. You have two options available to find these problems:

1. Go through the logical steps of the program to see the state of variables step by step.
2. Use the debugger to analyze and extract the logic of the program.

In SAP, you can debug any ABAP program, whether it's custom developed or a standard program. This section provides tips, tricks, and techniques to improve your experience when using the ABAP Debugger and make it easier to analyze and find bugs in your ABAP programs.

Tip (37)

Using SAP GUI Shortcuts to Debug Popup Windows

You can switch on debugging for popup windows by creating an SAP shortcut file for command /h and dragging this file onto a popup window.

Normally, if you know the place in the source code that you want to debug, you can easily place a breakpoint there, and a debugger will be triggered when you execute the program and the position that you marked is reached. You can also switch on debugging at any screen by entering the /h command into the command field on the SAP GUI toolbar. However, you can't use the /h command to stop popup windows because there is no command field. In this tip, we'll show you how to bypass this problem by using SAP GUI shortcuts to trigger the /h command on popup windows.

✅ And Here's How ...

To switch on debugging for popup windows, you need to create an SAP GUI shortcut file. The SAP GUI shortcut is a file that can be used to execute transactions or system commands directly from a file.

You can use three different methods to create an SAP GUI shortcut, which we discuss in the following sections.

Method 1
Click the GENERATE A SHORTCUT button (🗒) on the SAP GUI toolbar. The window in Figure 1 appears; enter the details of the shortcut.

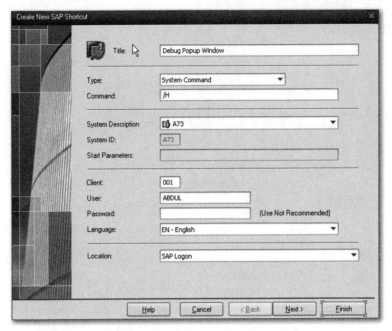

⋩ *Figure 1 Creating an SAP GUI Shortcut*

Follow these steps:

1. Enter a title in the TITLE field.
2. Select SYSTEM COMMAND from the TYPE dropdown.
3. Enter "/h" in the COMMAND field.
4. Click FINISH.

A shortcut file with an extension *.sap* is created on the desktop.

Method 2

1. Right-click on the Windows desktop.
2. Select NEW – SAP GUI SHORTCUT.
3. Enter the name of the file and press [Enter].
4. Right-click on the file, and select EDIT from the context menu.
5. Select SYSTEM COMMAND from the TYPE dropdown.
6. Enter "/h" in the COMMAND field.
7. Click OK.

Method 3

Create a text file named *Debugger.sap,* open it in any text editor (e.g., Notepad), and write the following text into the file:

```
[Function]
Command=/H
Title=Debugger
Type=SystemCommand
```

Debug the Popup

Now you have created a SAP GUI shortcut file. Open the popup window that you want to debug, and drag the shortcut file onto the popup as shown in Figure 2.

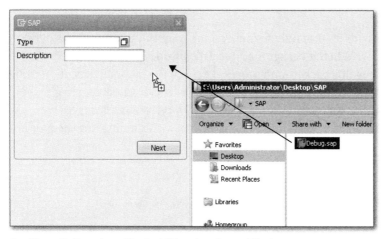

≫ *Figure 2 Dragging a Shortcut File onto a Popup Window*

When you drop the file on the popup window, you'll see the Debugging switched on message on the status bar. Now you can start the debugger tool by pressing the `Enter` key.

Tip 38

Debugging Background Jobs

You can debug a background job whether it's running, finished, or not started yet by using the same selection-screen parameters as when it was scheduled.

Background jobs are used mainly for scheduling long-running programs periodically or once only. When a background job fails or doesn't run as expected, you may need to debug this background process to check the program execution using the same selection-screen parameters used when it was scheduled. We'll show you how to use the tools available in the Job Overview and Process Overview transactions to debug a background process whether it's running, finished, or not yet started.

✓ And Here's How ...

You can debug background jobs in Transaction SM37 (Job Overview) and Transaction SM50 (Process Overview) according to the status of the job. You usually need to debug background processes when it's taking too much time to run or when it isn't running as expected. We'll discuss each of these transactions in the following sections.

Job Overview Transaction: Debugging Scheduled or Finished Background Jobs

You can debug a background job in the Job Overview transaction using the DEBUG JOB function, if the background job is in one of the following statuses:

▶ Scheduled
▶ Released
▶ Ready

- ▶ Finished
- ▶ Canceled

Access Transaction SM37 and select the relevant job as shown in Figure 1. Choose EXTRAS • DEBUG JOB to start the debugging process.

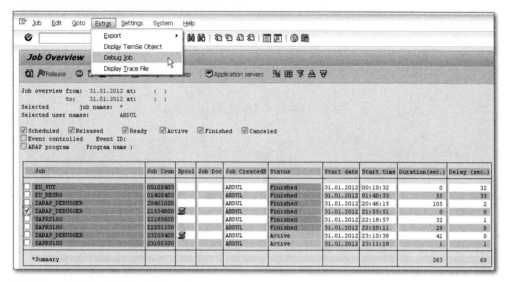

⤊ **Figure 1** Debug Jobs in Job Overview

An ABAP program opens in a debugger session. This is not the ABAP program that you actually wanted to debug, so you must step through a few times (you can use F7) to reach the code you need. You can see that selection-screen variables have the same values as when it was scheduled. You can now debug the program in the same conditions as when it was running in the background. Note that the program runs as it's running in the background, and the value of the SY-BATCH field will be "X" even if you run the program in the foreground.

Job Overview Transaction: Debugging Running Background Jobs

If the background job that you want to debug is running, you can debug it with Transaction SM37 using the CAPTURE ACTIVE JOB function.

Select the relevant job in Transaction SM37 and choose JOB • CAPTURE ACTIVE JOB to start the debugging process.

Now the running program stops in debug session, and you can step through the program to perform the debugging tasks. When you finish your debugging, you can release the program with the execute (F8) function.

Process Overview Transaction: Debugging Running Background Jobs

There's an alternative way of debugging running jobs in the Process Overview transaction (Transaction SM50). Process Overview allows you to see the details of processes running on the application server that you are logged on to. You can see both background and foreground processes in the list.

Select the job that you want to debug from the list as shown in Figure 2, and use the following menu path to start the debugging process:

ADMINISTRATION • PROGRAM • DEBUGGING

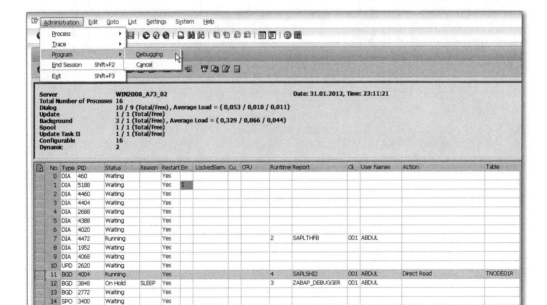

⤊ *Figure 2* Debug Running Processes in the Process Overview Transaction

Setting Breakpoints for ABAP Commands and Command Groups

You can set breakpoints for ABAP commands and command groups, and then program execution stops in the ABAP Debugger every time it reaches a given statement that you suspect will cause a problem.

When you debug a program with a complex logic to find a bug, it isn't easy to find a suitable starting point for debugging. You may have to step through the program line by line or try to step over the modules to find where the problem is originating. If you know or suspect that the problem might occur on a specific ABAP statement or around that statement, you can set a breakpoint for that ABAP statement and program execution stops in the debugger every time it reaches that statement. This will help you find the problem quickly without stepping through the source code line by line.

✅ And Here's How ...

The BREAKPOINT AT STATEMENT function is used to interrupt a program before the specified command or command group is executed. You need to enter into debug mode to use this function. When you're in debug mode for a specific program, use the following menu path to start the BREAKPOINT AT STATEMENT function:

BREAKPOINTS • BREAKPOINT AT • BREAKPOINT AT STATEMENT

You'll get a popup window with several tabs as shown in Figure 1.

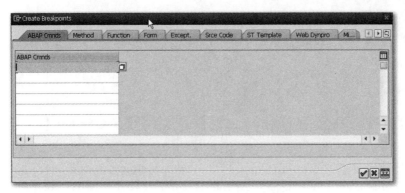

✿ *Figure 1 Create Breakpoints Popup*

The ABAP CMNDS tab is used to set breakpoints for commands and command groups. You can directly write your command or select it from the ⌷F4⌷ search help. Search help on this screen is available after SAP NetWeaver release 7.02. On the search help window, as shown in Figure 2, you'll see a list of commands and commands groups that can be selected to set a specific breakpoint.

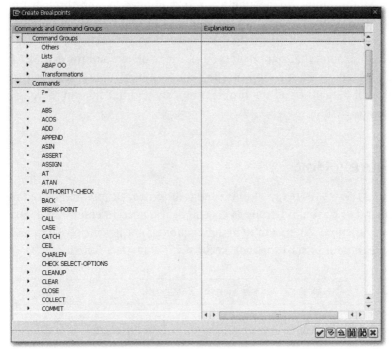

✿ *Figure 2 List of Commands and Command Groups*

As you can see in Figure 2, some commands have an expand button on the left. When you click this button, the variants of this command are listed, and you can also select the variants of the command instead of the command itself. For example, if you expand the CALL statement, you can select any of the underlying statements as shown in Figure 3.

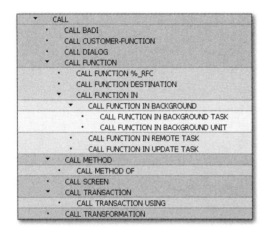

《 Figure 3 *Variant List for the CALL Command*

You can select any command from the list. If you select a command that has child nodes, the breakpoint is set for all child nodes as well. For example, if you select the statement CALL FUNCTION, the breakpoint is set for the following statements:

▶ CALL FUNCTION %_RFC

▶ CALL FUNCTION DESTINATION

▶ CALL FUNCTION IN BACKGROUND TASK

▶ CALL FUNCTION IN BACKGROUND UNIT

▶ CALL FUNCTION IN REMOTE TASK

▶ CALL FUNCTION IN UPDATE TASK

You can now run the program, and it will stop only at the statements that you set breakpoints for using this technique.

Using External Breakpoints to Debug External Calls

You can use external breakpoints to debug a program that's called externally via RFC or HTTP.

Breakpoints are used to interrupt the program execution and let you debug and analyze the ABAP program. If you set a session breakpoint in an ABAP program, the program execution stops, and the debugger session opens when the execution reaches the breakpoint position. However, if the program is called externally by an RFC or HTTP interface, the session breakpoints can't interrupt the program execution. In this tip, we'll show you how to use external breakpoints to debug programs that are called externally.

✓ And Here's How ...

Before you use external breakpoints, you need to adjust the debugging settings in the ABAP EDITOR tab of the USER-SPECIFIC SETTINGS window. Open this window by choosing UTILITIES • SETTINGS in the ABAP Workbench.

Figure 1 shows the settings that you can adjust for external debugging.

⌃ *Figure 1* Settings for External Debugging

Set the username of the person who will run the program externally. When the specified breakpoint is reached by this user, an ABAP Debugger starts in a new session, and you can start your debugging process from this point.[1]

This feature is extremely useful when you and the user that's starting the process are working at physically different locations. If an error is reported by an end user, and you want to debug the same case, you must first set the username of the end user in the USER-SPECIFIC SETTINGS window and set the breakpoint using the SET/ DELETE EXTERNAL BREAKPOINT button (⬛) on the toolbar in the ABAP Editor. Then tell the end user to run the program and wait without closing the current session. When the end user reaches the breakpoint, the ABAP DEBUGGER window is opened in your session and you take the control of the program. You can now debug, analyze the problem, and release the program after you finish.

Usually SAP systems have more than one application servers, and incoming requests are redirected to the appropriate application server determined by load balancing tools. External breakpoints are valid for the entire AS ABAP system by default. You can also set the validity of the breakpoint for only the current application server by using the ONLY CURRENT APPLICATIONSERVER checkbox on the DEBUGGING tab shown in Figure 1.

---

1 Both the user you specify here and the user you logged on to the system must be authorized for debugging.

Tip 41

Customizing the ABAP Debugger Desktop Tabs

You can modify and save your ABAP Debugger desktop tabs according to your own needs to improve your debugging process.

While you're debugging an ABAP program, there are several tools available in the ABAP Debugger that you can use for different debugging tasks. Each tool is placed on a different tab, and you need to navigate to the relevant tab to use these tools. There are also tools that are not displayed on any tab. To save time and make the process easier, we'll show you how to customize the DESKTOP 1, DESKTOP 2, and DESKTOP 3 tabs according to your own needs. You can add up to four of your most important or commonly used tools on each tab and save the layout as the default layout.

✔ And Here's How ...

Desktops are work areas that you can use to arrange the tools that you use frequently in the ABAP Debugger. You can customize these desktops according to your needs and navigate between desktops easily by changing the active tab. Let's consider an example; when you double click on an internal table variable in the source code, it's displayed on the Variable Fast Display tool, but you can't see the internal table contents. You must click on the variable name on the Variable Fast Display tool, but this time the active tab changes to the TABLES tool tab.

When you're in the middle of the debugging session and trying to analyze the many variables to find a bug, it isn't practical to navigate between the tabs. If you add the Table tool to the current desktop under the Variable Fast Display tool, it will be very easy to analyze the source code, variables, and tables on the same screen. To solve these problems, you can customize an ABAP Debugger desktop as shown in Figure 1.

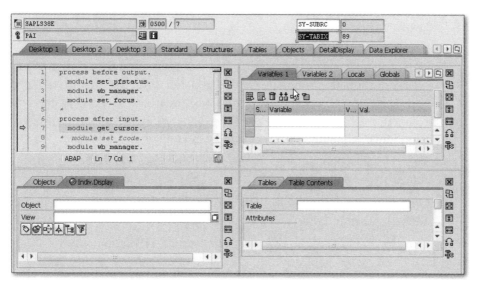

⋩ *Figure 1* An Example of an ABAP Debugger Desktop

Four tools are shown on the DESKTOP 1 tab: Source Code, Object, Variable Fast Display, and Table. You can remove any of these tools or swap the positions on the desktop using the vertical toolbar to the right of each tool. The following functions are available as buttons on the toolbar:

▸ CLOSE TOOL (⊠)
Removes the tool from the desktop.

▸ REPLACE TOOL (⬚)
Allows you to replace the tool by opening a NEW TOOL window from which you can select the new tool.

▸ FULL SCREEN (⬚)
Removes all other tools and expands the tool to the remaining area of the current desktop.

▸ MAXIMIZE VERTICALLY (⬚)
This function is available only when there is another tool on top or bottom of the tool. When you use this function, the other tool is removed, and the current tool expands vertically.

► MAXIMIZE HORIZONTALLY (⬌)

This function is available only when there is another tool on the left or right of the tool. When you use this function, the other tool is removed, and the current tool expands horizontally.

► SWAP (⟲)

This function allows you to swap the positions of tools on the desktop. When you select this function, a popup appears, and you can select the direction that you want to swap: VERTICALLY, HORIZONTALLY, or DIAGONALLY. Only the possible directions are displayed on the popup. For example, if you have only three tools as shown in Figure 2, you select the swap tool on the following:

❶: Vertical and diagonal swap aren't possible. Hence, Tool ❶ immediately moves to the right, and Tool ❷ and Tool ❸ are moved to the left.

❷: Diagonal swap isn't possible. Hence, the popup appears, and you can select between vertical or horizontal swap.

❸: Same as Tool ❷. You can select between vertical or horizontal swap.

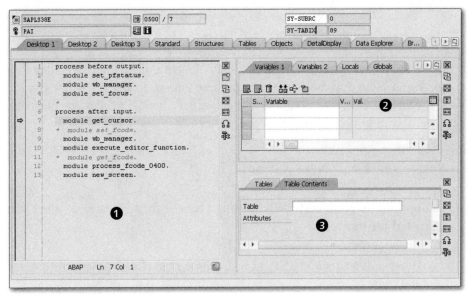

⌃ *Figure 2* Debugger Desktop with Three Tools

► SERVICES OF THE TOOL (▦)

When you click on this function, the system displays the services that are available for the selected tool. Each tool has its own specific services. For example, when you select this function for the Variable Fast Display tool, the available services are displayed as shown in Figure 3.

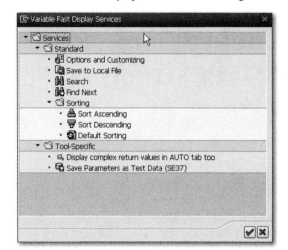

≪ *Figure 3* *Services of the Variable Fast Display Tool*

Changes you make are valid only on the current session. If you want to make the changes permanent, you need to save them using the SAVE LAYOUT button (🔲Layout) on the toolbar.

Tip 42

Using the Diff Tool to Compare Complex ABAP Data Structures

You can use the Diff tool during your debugging process to compare two complex ABAP data structures with respect to their type or value.

When you're debugging an ABAP program, you may need to compare the types or values of two variables, structures, internal tables, or even object instances. This isn't a big issue if you want to compare two simple types or structures with a few fields. However, when you want to compare more complex data structures, it becomes difficult using the basic debugger tools. Luckily, the Diff tool allows you to compare two ABAP data structures, simple data types, strings, or ABAP objects and see the differences with respect to their values and types.

✅ And Here's How ...

Imagine that you have two internal tables with hundreds of lines or two objects with a complex structure. Trying to compare these elements using the traditional ABAP Debugger tools would be a nightmare. Here, you can easily use the Diff tool to compare and see the differences.

You can access the Diff tool from the DIFF tab in the ABAP Debugger. You can also add it to any of the customizable desktops. The Diff tool has two fields—VARIABLE 1 and VARIABLE 2—where you can enter the name of the variables to compare. Alternatively, and more easily, you can start the Diff tool directly in the default debugger desktop. Using the Variable Fast Display tool, select two variables and click the START COMPARISON button on the toolbar as shown in Figure 1.

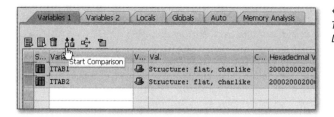

« *Figure 1* *Starting the Diff Tool from the Variable Fast Display Tool*

After you click the START COMPARISON button, the two variables are automatically transferred to the Diff tool. If there's a Diff tool on the same desktop, the variables are transferred to this tool; otherwise, they are transferred to the default Diff tool on a separate tab.

Figure 2 illustrates a sample comparison result of two internal tables.

Desktop 1	Desktop 2	Desktop 3	Standard	Structures	Tables	Objects	DetailDisplay	Data Explorer	Break./Watchpoints	Diff	Script

History | Compare ABAP Variables

Variable 1 ITAB1   Val. [2x4(64)]Standard Table
Variable 2 ITAB2   Val. [2x3(60)]Standard Table
Start Comparison   Max. No. of Hits   100

Index	Diff	G...	Description	Location	ITAB1	ITAB2
1			Different Number of Columns	ITAB1	4	3
2			Different Row Length	ITAB1	64	60
3			Component Missing	ITAB1-F4	F4	
4			Type Difference: No Value Comparison Possible	ITAB1		

⌃ *Figure 2* *Comparison Result of Two Internal Tables with Different Structures*

As you can see in Figure 2, the internal tables don't have the same structure, so a value comparison isn't possible. The list only has the results of the type comparison. In Figure 3, you can see the comparison result of internal tables that have the same structure.

Desktop 1	Desktop 2	Desktop 3	Standard	Structures	Tables	Objects	DetailDisplay	Data Explorer	Break./Watchpoints	Diff	Script

History | Compare ABAP Variables

Variable 1 ITAB1   Val. [2x3(60)]Standard Table
Variable 2 ITAB2   Val. [2x3(60)]Standard Table
Start Comparison   Max. No. of Hits   100

Index	Diff	G...	Description	Location	ITAB1	ITAB2
1			The elements have different contents	ITAB1[1]-F2+0(4)	2222	XXXX
2			The elements have different contents	ITAB1[2]-F2+0(4)	XXXX	BBBB

⌃ *Figure 3* *Comparison Result of Two Internal Tables with the Same Structure*

139

This time, the values of the internal tables are also compared, and the elements that have different values are listed in the result set. If you click the DISPLAY VARIABLES (🔍) button just above the list, two Table tools are automatically added into the desktop, and the contents of internal tables are listed in these tables as shown in Figure 4.

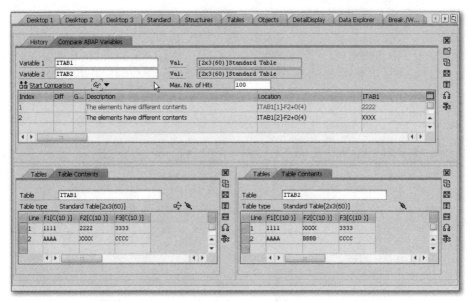

⯅ *Figure 4 Displaying Table Contents in the Diff Tool*

The HISTORY tab in the Diff tool shows you the list of the comparisons that you made so far in the current session. This feature helps you easily go back to the previous comparisons.

Tip 43

Viewing and Manipulating Internal Tables Using the Table Tool

You can use the Table tool to view and manipulate the contents of internal tables in the ABAP Debugger.

When you're analyzing an ABAP program in the debugger, you often need to analyze the internal tables, modify the contents, or even add new lines into the table. Internal tables are used excessively in ABAP programming, and being able to analyze and manipulate internal tables easily in the debugger can be very helpful in your debugging tasks. You can perform all of these tasks easily by using the Table tool in the ABAP Debugger.

✔ And Here's How ...

The ABAP Debugger has a Table tool on a separate tab that allows you to display or modify the contents of internal tables in the debugging session. You can also add this tool to any of the debugger desktops to use it more efficiently.

While debugging an ABAP program, navigate to the TABLES tab, and enter the name of the internal table variable into the TABLE field in the TABLE CONTENTS tab to see the contents as shown in Figure 1.

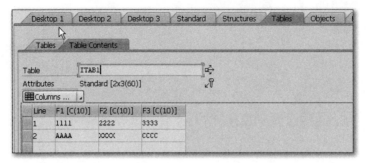

⌃ *Figure 1* *Displaying Internal Table Contents in the Table Tool*

You can see the history of the internal tables that you displayed in the current session on the TABLES tab.

You can also navigate the Table tool by double-clicking on the internal table name in the Variable Fast Display tool in the ABAP Debugger. However, if the internal table has a header line, the debugger navigates to the Structures tool instead of the Table tool. This time, you can click the TABLE icon (▦) on the left of the internal table name in the Variable Fast Display tool to navigate to the Table tool as shown in Figure 2.

⌃ *Figure 2* *The Variable Fast Display Tool Can Be Used to Navigate to the Table Tool*

You can also add the Table tool to any of the desktops if you use it often, as described in Tip 41. You can see the final result in Figure 3.

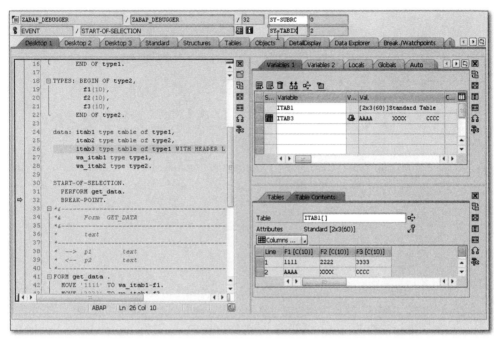

⋀ **Figure 3** *Adding the Table Tool into Debugger Desktop*

This time, if you double-click on the internal table name, the content is displayed in the Table tool directly instead of navigating to the Table tool on a separate tab. However, if the internal table has a header line, you again have to click on the TABLE icon or enter the name of the internal table into the Table tool directly.

The SERVICE menu for the Table tool can be accessed using the SERVICES OF THE TOOL (🔲) button on the right toolbar. A popup opens, and you can select the service that you want to use from the list of services. You can use these services to import, export, and modify the internal table contents.

You can also access all of these functions using the context menu of the Table tool. The functions under the COLUMNS section can also be accessed using the COLUMNS button (🔲 Columns ... ◢) just above the internal table contents.

Note that the SERVICES list in your system may not include all of the services listed here depending on which SAP NetWeaver version you're using.

Tip (44)

Saving Test Data for Function Modules in the ABAP Debugger

You can save the import parameters of a function module in a test data directory during a debug session so that you can use the parameters again later.

Imagine that you're debugging an ABAP program and figure out that the problem has originated from a function module. If the function module has a complex logic, the best option is to debug it separately in the Function Builder. However, you must use the same import parameters that are used in the calling program to reproduce the error. In this tip, we'll show you how to save the import parameters while in a function module to a test data directory during the debug session and use them later in Function Builder to test the function module individually.

✓ And Here's How ...

The Variable Fast Display tool in the ABAP Debugger allows you to view and modify (if possible) the variables used in the ABAP program. If you're in a function module, you can save the current values of the import parameters into a test data directory of a function module. You can use the SAVE PARAMETERS AS TEST DATA function in the TOOL-SPECIFIC services list in the VARIABLE FAST DISPLAY SERVICES list as shown in Figure 1.

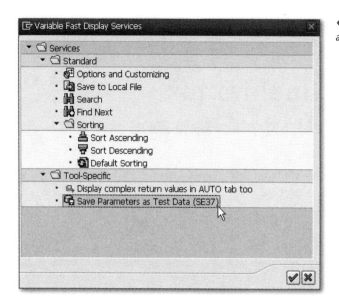

≪ Figure 1 Save Parameters
as Test Data

After you select the SAVE PARAMETERS AS TEST DATA function, enter the name of the
test data in the popup as shown in Figure 2 and click the CONTINUE button (✔).

≪ Figure 2 Popup to Enter
the Name of the Test Data

All parameters are saved, and you can access this test data using the TEST DATA
DIRECTORY button on the TEST FUNCTION MODULE screen in the Function Builder
(Transaction SE37).

Using Watchpoints to Monitor Variable Changes

You can use watchpoints to monitor and find changed or altered variables during a debugging session and then interrupt the program.

When you debug an ABAP program, you sometimes realize that one of the critical variables is changed suddenly in one of the modules (subroutine, function module, class, etc.) that you step over instead of stepping into the module, and this change may be the main reason for the problem that you are analyzing. It may not be easy to step into the module source code and go step by step to find the exact position where the variable is changed because the module you want to debug is too big. You can use watchpoints in that case to monitor the variable, interrupt the program execution, and open a debugger session when this variable is changed.

✓ And Here's How ...

You can create a watchpoint while you're in the ABAP Debugger using the CREATE WATCHPOINT (⬜ Watchpoint) button on the toolbar. It will open a popup window, where you can enter the details of the watchpoint that you want to create. Two types of watchpoints can be created according to your requirement:

▸ WATCHPOINT AT VARIABLE
  Monitors the variable during the program run and stops immediately when the value of variable changes.

▸ WATCHPOINT AT OBJECT ATTRIBUTE
  Monitors the object during the program run and stops immediately when one of the selected attributes of the object changes.

For example, suppose you have an internal Table ITAB1 in your program, and you want to find the position where the second record is appended into the table. You can create a watchpoint by filling in settings in the CREATE WATCHPOINT window as shown in Figure 1.

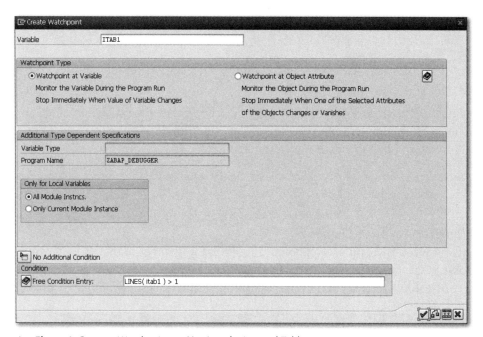

⌃ *Figure 1* *Create a Watchpoint to Monitor the Internal Table*

Enter the name of the internal table in the VARIABLE field, and select the WATCH-POINT TYPE as WATCHPOINT AT VARIABLE.

Create a Watchpoint for a Local Variable
If you're creating a watchpoint for a local variable in a module, you can select whether you want to create a watchpoint for the current module instance or for all instances.

In the FREE CONDITION ENTRY field, you can enter the condition for the watch-point. If you don't enter any condition, the ABAP Debugger stops on any changes on the variable. Otherwise, it stops only if the variable is changed and the specified condition is met. The syntax of the conditions is identical to the ABAP syntax. In our example, you would write the following condition to interrupt the program on the second append to the internal table:

```
LINES( itab1 ) > 1
```

This is the same syntax that you use to check the lines of the internal table in ABAP. The condition you write must comply with the following syntax:

```
<Function(variable) or variable or literal>
Operator
<Function(variable) or variable or literal>
```

You can check the syntax of the condition using the CHECK (🔐) button on the toolbar.

Finally, you can click the CONTINUE ✅ button to create the watchpoint and close the window, or you can click the TRANSFER button (⏬) to stay on the CREATE WATCHPOINT popup create a new watchpoint.

Now you've created the watchpoint, so the debugger will stop when the condition you specify is met.

Monitor Attribute Changes

If you want to create a watchpoint to monitor the changes to the attributes of an object, select the WATCHPOINT TYPE as WATCHPOINT AT OBJECT ATTRIBUTE and the ADDITIONAL TYPE DEPENDENT SPECIFICATIONS changes as shown in Figure 2.

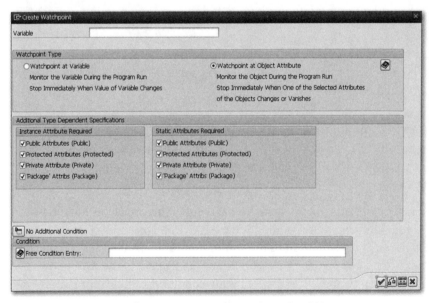

❯ **Figure 2** Create a Watchpoint to Monitor the Attribute of an Object

Now you can set which type of attributes you want to monitor: instance or static attributes. For each one, you can select the visibility of the attributes: PUBLIC, PROTECTED, PRIVATE, and PACKAGE.

You can see the watchpoints you've created by viewing the BREAK./WATCHPOINTS tab in the ABAP Debugger as shown in Figure 3.

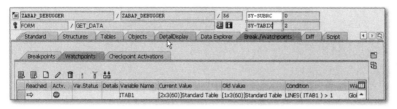

⤊ *Figure 3* *Displaying Watchpoints in the ABAP Debugger*

You can perform the following operations on this screen:

▶ Create, modify, or delete a watchpoint

▶ Activate or deactivate a watchpoint

▶ Compare variables

The COMPARE VARIABLES (🔀) function allows you to compare the initial condition of the monitored variable with the current condition in the Diff tool. The comparison result will be displayed as shown in Figure 4.

⤊ *Figure 4* *Using the Diff Tool to Compare the Current Value with the Initial Value*

Be careful when using watchpoints for internal tables that have too many records. When you create a watchpoint, the system creates the copy of an object and uses this copy to monitor the changes. If the internal table you're monitoring is too large, keeping the duplicate copy of this table can lead to high memory consumption. You can try to keep this type of watchpoint for short program durations.

Tip 46

Using Debugger Scripting to Analyze Complex Debugging Scenarios[1]

You can use the Debugger Scripting tool to implement custom debugging tasks by writing a local ABAP class and taking the control from the ABAP Debugger.

Although the ABAP Debugger has great features that allow you to debug and analyze an ABAP program, you may still have complex cases that the standard tools offered by the ABAP Debugger can't solve. The Debugger Scripting tool helps you in such cases by allowing you to use scripting options to implement your custom requirements in the ABAP Debugger.

✅ And Here's How ...

Access the Debugger Scripting tool by selecting the SCRIPT tab on the far right side of the ABAP Debugger. Figure 1 shows the initial screen of the tool.

A default script template is loaded in the editor by default, and you can write any ABAP object-oriented (OO) statements here. There are four methods defined in the class:

▶ `prologue`
Generates the ABAP source handler class `abap_source`, which handles access to the source code and variables in the program that you are debugging. Runs only when you start the script.

---

1   Applicable to SAP NetWeaver release 7.3 and later.

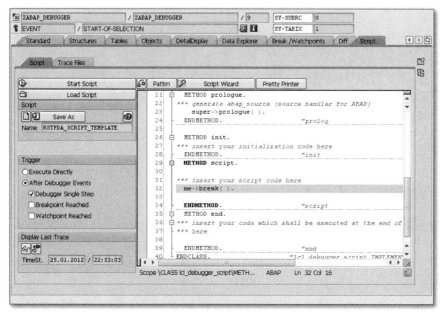

⋀ *Figure 1* Initial View of the Debugger Scripting Tool

▶ init

Runs only when you start the script. You can write any initialization code here.

▶ script

Runs every time the debugger is expected to stop. You can implement your logic in this method to change the behavior of the debugger.

▶ end

Runs when you end the script.

Notice that this is just a local ABAP class implementation. You can also add your own methods in the class. Normally, you can implement your whole logic only in the method `script`, but you can also use the other methods if you're implementing an advanced logic. If you look into the default template, you can see that there is only one line in the `script` method:

```
me->break( ).
```

This is nothing but the normal breakpoint command. Let's start using the tool with the default script template to understand the basics of the tool.

On the left side of the editor, you can adjust the stop condition using the trigger options. Choose one or more options from the following:

▶ EXECUTE DIRECTLY
The script is executed immediately with the current conditions.

▶ AFTER DEBUGGING EVENTS
The script is run after the selected trigger events are reached. You can select any of the following three triggers:

   ▶ DEBUGGER SINGLE STEP
   If you select this trigger, the debugger runs a single step in the source code. This is the same as using the single step function (F5) in the normal debugging scenario.

   ▶ BREAKPOINT REACHED
   If you select this trigger, the debugger script runs every time the breakpoint condition is reached. The CHANGE button also appears if you select this option and allows you to open the Breakpoints tool at the bottom of the screen. You can modify breakpoint conditions with this tool.

   ▶ WATCHPOINT REACHED
   If you select this trigger, the debugger script runs every time the watchpoint condition is reached. The CHANGE button also appears if you select this option and allows you to open the Watchpoints tool at the bottom of the screen. You can modify watchpoint conditions with this tool.

Start the script by using the START SCRIPT button on the left. The debugger behaves exactly the same as the normal debugging scenario because there is only a break statement in the script. The script stops on the trigger condition and waits for user action.

If you select CONTINUE SCRIPT, the ABAP program will be executed to the next trigger condition and again stops. You can use the EXIT SCRIPT button whenever you want to stop the execution of the script. The `script` method is executed at each stop, and the `end` method is executed when you exit the script.

So far, we've used only the default script template to see the basics of the tool. Now, let's go one step further and see how you can benefit from the tool and handle the custom debugging scenarios.

Click the SCRIPT WIZARD button just above the editor window on the tool. The SCRIP WIZARD window opens showing the DEBUGGER SCRIPT SERVICES list from which you can select the predefined script services that you can insert into the script. The script services are grouped in categories as shown in Figure 2. As you see, there are several categories, and each category has many script services that you can use for different purposes.

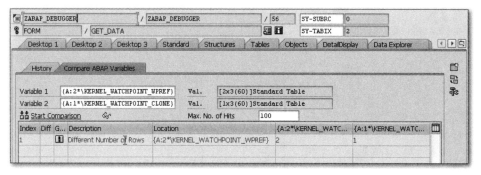

⊼ *Figure 2* *Script Wizard Window*

You can insert any script service from the list by double-clicking it. Predefined debugger scripts also can be defined using the LOAD SCRIPT button on the left side of the editor. Click on the LOAD SCRIPT button, and select the script using the search help in the SCRIPT NAME field on the LOAD DEBUGGER SCRIPT popup window. You can also load a script from the local file by selecting the LOCAL FILE as SCRIPT SOURCE.

Now click the OVERVIEW OF DEBUGGER SCRIPTS button (⬚). An OBJECT BROWSER window opens providing an overview of debugger scripts. Select the script from the collection categorized by the topic as shown in Figure 3.

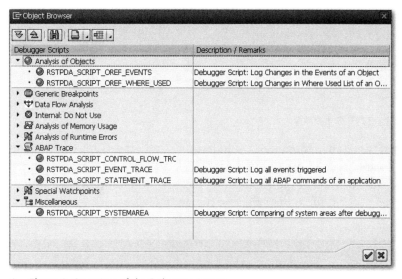

⊼ *Figure 3* *Overview of the Debugger Scripts*

Tip 47

Debugging Specific Program Areas Using the Software Layer-Aware Debugger[1]

You can debug specific parts of your code or jump from one point to another in the ABAP Debugger with a specific tool.

Imagine that you want to debug a big program but are only interested in a specific part of the program. This would be very easy if you knew the first access point of the layer that you're interested in. However, if you aren't sure about that point, you have to step through many lines of code to find it, which is tedious, time consuming, and error prone. However, the solution to your problem arrives in the form of the Software Layer-Aware Debugger tool. We'll explain how it allows you to define the profile for the layer that you're interested in and jump directly to that layer in the ABAP Debugger.

✓ And Here's How ...

Create object sets in Transaction SLAD, and put these object sets into a profile to use in the Software Layer-Aware Debugger tool. Select the OBJECT SETS tab on the initial screen, and click CREATE to create an object set. When the CREATE OBJECT SET popup screen opens, fill in the values as shown in Figure 1.

---

1 Applicable to SAP NetWeaver release 7.3 and later.

⌃ *Figure 1* Create Object Set Dialog

Object sets and object profiles are managed by the transport management system; you must create them in the customer namespace and put them into the appropriate packages. You may assign it to an APPLICATION COMPONENT, but it isn't mandatory.

Click the CONTINUE button (✅) and an empty object set is created as shown in Figure 2. This lets you create selection sets to define the object set.

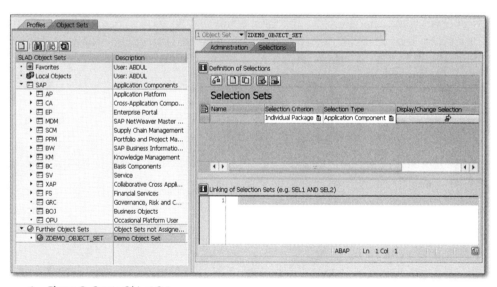

⌃ *Figure 2* Create Object Set

Object sets are defined using selection sets and selection set expressions. You can define the following object types in a selection set:

▶ Individual package

▶ Package with subpackage

- ▸ Program/class
- ▸ Function module
- ▸ Implemented interface

Perform the following steps to create a selection set:

1. Click the CREATE (□) or INSERT buttons (□) to add a new selection set.
2. Enter the name of the selection set.
3. Select the SELECTION CRITERION.
4. Select the SELECTION TYPE. Select APPLICATION COMPONENT if you want to select objects from the application hierarchy. Otherwise, select SELECTION SCREEN to specify the name of the objects in a selection screen.
5. Click the DISPLAY/CHANGE SELECTION button and select the objects that you want to include in a selection set. An object selection screen opens according to the selection type that you defined in the previous step.

After creating the selection sets, link them using AND, OR, and NOT operations in the LINKING OF SELECTION SETS area if you've defined more than one selection set. The link condition for all selection sets must be defined here.

Suppose that you defined the following selection sets:

- ▸ ZAG: All objects included in Package ZAG.
- ▸ ZAGF: All function modules starting with ZAG_*.

And suppose that the following three function modules are called in the transaction that you are going to debug:

- ▸ ZAN_DETAIL (Package ZAG)
- ▸ ZAG_SEARCH (Package ZAG)
- ▸ ZAG_CREATE (Package ZMM)

Table 1 shows the stop conditions for each function on different cases.

LINK	ZAN_DETAIL	ZAG_SEARCH	ZAG_CREATE
ZAG AND ZAGF	NO	STOP	NO
ZAG OR ZAGF	STOP	STOP	STOP
ZAG AND NOT ZAGF	STOP	NO	NO

⌃ *Table 1 Different Stop Conditions in Different Link Options*

As you can see, you can create many combinations for different cases using the link feature. When you finish linking selection sets, click the CHECK button (![icon]) to check the whole object set to see if there are any errors. Finally, save the object set if there are no errors.

Now, create the object profile. Navigate to the PROFILES tab and click the CREATE button (![icon]). When the CREATE PROFILE popup opens, fill in the values as shown in Figure 3.

≫ *Figure 3 Create Profile Dialog*

After you click the CREATE PROFILE button (![icon]), an empty profile is created as shown in Figure 4. You can insert object sets into the empty profile.

≫ *Figure 4 Create Profile*

Now use the CREATE button (![icon]) or INSERT button (![icon]) to add the object sets that you created in the previous step into the profile. Note that there's a predefined object set <<%REST%>> which specifies the ABAP code that resides outside of the object sets you defined. You can remove it if you don't want to stop on the rest of the code in the debugger. The following characteristics can be defined for each object set, including the predefined object set <<%REST%>>:

► VISIBLE

The selected object set is visible in the debugger when you select this checkbox. If you clear this checkbox, the relevant object set won't be visible, and the debugger won't stop when you use the normal debugging steps. For example, if you clear the VISIBLE checkbox for the predefined object set <<%REST%>>, you can only see the visible selection sets in the debugger, and the rest of the code is skipped even if you step in using the single step ($\boxed{\text{F5}}$) function.

► POINT OF ENTRY

The debugger stops when the specified object set is reached.

► POINT OF EXIT

The debugger stops when the specified object set is exited.

► INCLUDING SYSTEM CODE

The system programs in the object set are also included in the profile.

When you finish defining the profile, you're ready to use it in the ABAP Debugger. Open the program that you want to debug, and start in debug mode. When you are in the debugger, click the CONFIGURE DEBUGGER LAYER button to open the LAYER-AWARE DEBUGGER SETTINGS popup. Select the LAYER-AWARE DEBUGGER ACTIVE checkbox to activate the tool. Then select the USE OF PREDEFINED OBJECT SET (LAYER) USING DEBUGGER PROFILE radio button to define the profile to use for the Software Layer-Aware Debugging tool. Select the profile that you created in the previous step, and click the CONTINUE button (✅). Now you can use the NEXT OBJECT SET button. Whenever you click the NEXT OBJECT SET button, the debugger jumps to the next object set. If you step through with the single step function ($\boxed{\text{F5}}$), the debugger stops only in the visible part of the code.

Using Conditional Breakpoints to Check Specific Conditions[1]

You can use conditional breakpoints when you want to set a breakpoint that is active for a specific condition only.

Breakpoints are used frequently to stop the execution of the program on a specific line and analyze that part of the code. However, sometimes the program may hit the same breakpoint several times in a loop, which makes it very hard to check the status of the variables at each step to see if the desired condition is met, especially when the loop is repeated a large number of times. In this tip, we'll show you how to specify a condition for a breakpoint to configure it to stop only in that condition.

✓ And Here's How ...

When you set a breakpoint on a line inside a loop, it will obviously stop on each loop. If the loop runs a large number of times, this breakpoint becomes meaningless because it will take too much time to step through each step to analyze the program.

After setting a breakpoint in the source code, you can specify a condition for a breakpoint in the ABAP Debugger by right-clicking on the breakpoint on the left side and selecting the CREATE BREAKPOINT CONDITION option as shown in Figure 1.

---

1 Applicable to SAP NetWeaver release 7.3 and later.

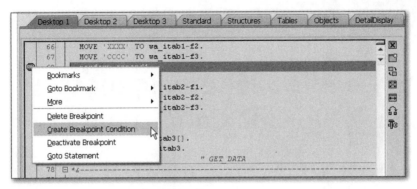

≋ *Figure 1 Creating a Breakpoint Condition*

The BREAKPOINT CONDITION popup opens; enter the condition as shown in Figure 2.

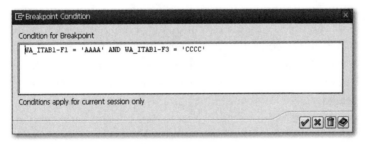

≋ *Figure 2 Specifying a Breakpoint Condition*

When you click CONTINUE (✓), the condition is saved and the debugger will stop only when the given condition is met.

Conditions can be created by using comparisons and operands that are logically linked with AND, OR, and NOT. These operands can be used in the following conditions:

- Variables
- Literals
- Debugger symbols
- Debugger functions

You can access the detailed explanation of the syntax of the breakpoint conditions using the DISPLAY HELP (◈) button on the BREAKPOINT CONDITION popup.

When you create the condition, the syntax check is performed, but the validity of the operands isn't checked. If the operand isn't valid, the warning message "Breakpoint condition cannot be evaluated at position 1" is displayed on the status bar, indicating that there's an error in the condition.

Breakpoint conditions are valid only for debugger breakpoints. If you save a breakpoint as a session or external breakpoint, the breakpoint condition won't be saved with it.

Tip (49)

Using Forward Navigation Features in the ABAP Debugger[1]

You can change forward navigation features in the ABAP Debugger to display the variable of your choice in the relevant Detailed Display or Data Explorer tools.

The Variable Fast Display tool in ABAP Debugger displays only the basic information for the complex variables such as internal tables and classes. When you double-click on a complex variable in the Variable Fast Display tool, the system opens the tool associated with the type of the variable on a separate desktop to display the detailed information for the variable. For example, when you click on the internal table variable, the Table tool opens on a separate desktop. However, it isn't practical to navigate between the tabs if you're using this feature several times for internal tables, structures, or objects. You can change this forward navigation behavior according to your preferences in the Variable Fast Display tool.

✓ And Here's How ...

When you double-click on a variable in the source code, it's displayed in the Variable Fast Display tool. However, if the variable is complex (internal table, structure, object, etc.), you must open it in the relevant Detailed Display tool by double-clicking the variable name in the Variable Fast Display tool.

You can configure the behavior of this feature using the SUSPEND NAVIGATION button (🗔) on the toolbar of the Variable Fast Display tool. When you click this button, two combo boxes appear near the button as shown in the Figure 1.

---

1 Applicable to SAP NetWeaver release 7.3 and later.

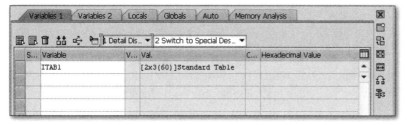

⚒ *Figure 1* *Configuring Forward Navigation in the Variable Fast Display Tool*

In the first combo box, choose one of the following two options to configure the tool that will be used to display the variable:

▶ DETAIL DISPLAY
The variable is displayed in the relevant Detailed Display tool. For example, internal tables are displayed in the Table tool, and structures are displayed in the Structure tool.

▶ DATA EXPLORER
The variable is displayed in Data Explorer, which displays objects, tables, and deep structures hierarchically.

In the second combo box, choose how the relevant tool will be opened:

▶ REPRESENTATION ON CURRENT DESKTOP
The relevant tool is opened on the current desktop. If there are already four tools on the desktop, a popup appears as shown in Figure 2, and you can choose which tool should be swapped with the new tool.

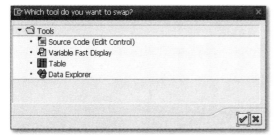

« *Figure 2* *Swap a Current Tool with the New Tool*

▶ SWITCH TO SPECIAL DESKTOP
The tool is opened on a separate debugger desktop.

▶ SWAP CURRENT TOOL
The current tool will be replaced with the new tool.

You may also want to skip the Variable Fast Display tool and open the relevant tool directly when you double-click a variable in the source code. This time, you can configure this behavior by choosing SETTINGS • CUSTOMIZING.

Configure the forward navigation feature on the GENERAL tab by selecting DISPLAY VARIABLE DIRECTLY IN THE RELEVANT DETAIL VIEW in the VARIABLE NAVIGATION FROM EDITOR field.

Analyzing Deep Nested Objects in the Main Object

You can analyze subcomponents of deep nested objects and structures in a tree without navigating away from the main object by using the Data Explorer tool.

When you're debugging an ABAP program, you can use the standard ABAP Debugger tools to analyze these variables if you aren't using ABAP objects and flat structures. For example, you can display the object details in the Objects tool and the structure fields in the Structures tool. However, if you have complex ABAP objects or nested structures, it can be difficult to navigate between the subcomponents and their relevant tools to analyze the top-level main object. In this tip, we'll show you how to use the Data Explorer tool to analyze the complex objects and structures in the ABAP Debugger.

✓ And Here's How ...

The Data Explorer tool is located on a separate tab in the ABAP Debugger. You can also add it into any of the debugger desktops to use it with other debugger tools.

Let's consider an example of using the Data Explorer tool to see the contents of the complex ABAP object:

1. Open `SALV_DEMO_TABLE_SIMPLE` in the ABAP Editor.
2. Navigate to the `display_fullscreen` part, and put a breakpoint on the `gr_table->display( )` statement.
3. Execute the program with default selection parameters. The program stops in the ABAP Debugger on the breakpoint.

4. Double-click on the GR_TABLE variable. The Variable Fast Display tool displays the basic information about the variable as shown in Figure 1.

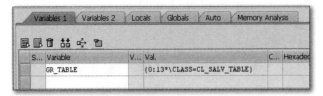

⌃ *Figure 1 Basic Display of the Object in the Variable Fast Display Tool*

5. Double-click on the GR_TABLE in the Variable Fast Display tool. Now you can see the object details in the Object tool as shown in Figure 2.

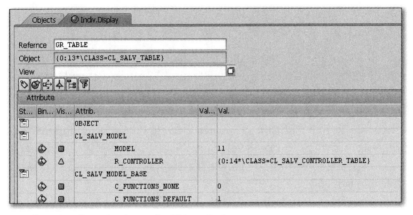

⌃ *Figure 2 Object Display in the Objects Tool*

This is the classic method to analyze the object in the ABAP Debugger. In Figure 2, notice that the subcomponent R_CONTROLLER is also an object, and you can't see the object members directly on the tool.

Now, let's go to the Data Explorer tool to display GR_TABLE in a better way:

1. Navigate to the DATA EXPLORER tab on the ABAP Debugger.

2. Enter "GR_TABLE" in the NAME field, and press Enter to open the object details in a tree structure as shown in Figure 3.

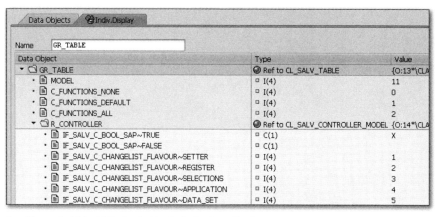

Data Objects	Indiv.Display		

Name GR_TABLE

Data Object	Type	Value
▼ GR_TABLE	Ref to CL_SALV_TABLE	{O:13*\CLA
• MODEL	I(4)	11
• C_FUNCTIONS_NONE	I(4)	0
• C_FUNCTIONS_DEFAULT	I(4)	1
• C_FUNCTIONS_ALL	I(4)	2
▼ R_CONTROLLER	Ref to CL_SALV_CONTROLLER_MODEL {O:14*\CLA
• IF_SALV_C_BOOL_SAP~TRUE	C(1)	X
• IF_SALV_C_BOOL_SAP~FALSE	C(1)	
• IF_SALV_C_CHANGELIST_FLAVOUR~SETTER	I(4)	1
• IF_SALV_C_CHANGELIST_FLAVOUR~REGISTER	I(4)	2
• IF_SALV_C_CHANGELIST_FLAVOUR~SELECTIONS	I(4)	3
• IF_SALV_C_CHANGELIST_FLAVOUR~APPLICATION	I(4)	4
• IF_SALV_C_CHANGELIST_FLAVOUR~DATA_SET	I(4)	5

☆ *Figure 3* Object Display in the Data Explorer Tool

Now you can see that the components of the complex members can also be displayed on the same screen. You can also display directly nested structures and internal tables on the tool without navigating away to the subcomponents. This saves your time and helps you focus on debugging tasks instead of navigating between variables.

Part 6

Analysis Tools

Things You'll Learn in this Section

The ABAP Workbench offers more than just great tools to develop enterprise applications for ABAP developers; it also provides test and analysis tools to help developers increase their productivity. These tools also help system administrators to analyze the technical problems encountered by end users. In this part of the book, you'll learn tips and tricks on how to use these different analysis tools.

Performing Detailed Checks on ABAP Programs with Extended Program Check

You can use the Extended Program Check utility to perform detailed code checks to prevent possible problems in ABAP programs before releasing them.

When you're developing an ABAP program, it's a good practice to perform a detailed check on the source code before releasing it to the quality or production system to make sure that it doesn't contain any obsolete, superfluous, or ugly statements. Even if you're an advanced ABAP programmer, sometimes your focus may move to the logic of the program, and you may use some obsolete statements or forget some messy declarations in the source code.

You may frequently use the SYNTAX CHECK function to check the program syntactically, but be aware that it only performs basic checks that can be run immediately in the ABAP Editor. You can also use the Extended Program Check utility to perform more detailed checks on the source code, as well as improve the quality of your ABAP programs. This utility will also show you better usages of the statements according to the programming guidelines, which will improve your ABAP knowledge and help you develop a habit of programming according to the programming guidelines.

And Here's How ...

The Extended Program Check utility allows you to perform detailed checks on the ABAP programs. You can access Extended Program Check using Transaction SLIN or by using the following menu path while you're in the ABAP Editor:

PROGRAM • CHECK • EXTENDED PROGRAM CHECK

In the selection screen that opens, you can select the checks that you want to perform as shown in Figure 1.

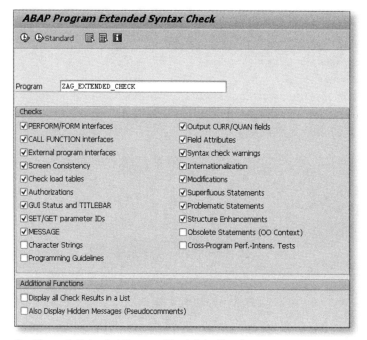

⌃ *Figure 1 Extended Program Check Selection-Screen*

Run the program by clicking the PERFORM CHECK (⏱) button. The selected checks are run on the source code, and the result is displayed in a table as shown in Figure 2.

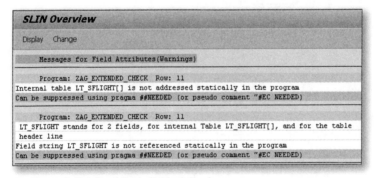

SLIN Overview

Display Results   Display All Results   Display Single Test

Check for Program ZAG_EXTENDED_CHECK	Errors	Warnings	Messages
Test Environment	0	0	0
PERFORM/FORM Interfaces	0	0	0
CALL FUNCTION interfaces	0	0	0
GUI Status and TITLEBAR	0	0	0
SET/GET Parameter IDs	0	0	0
Character Strings	0	0	3
Output CURR/QUAN fields	0	0	0
Field Attributes	0	2	0
Superfluous Statements	0	0	0
Syntax check warnings	2	0	0
Modifications	0	0	0
Problematic Statements	0	0	0
Programming Guidelines	0	3	0
Obsolete Statements	0	2	0
Hidden Errors and Warnings	0	0	0

⌃ *Figure 2* Extended Program Check Output

You can see the number of errors, warnings, and other messages on the table and navigate to the details of these messages by double-clicking on the number. The details are displayed as shown in Figure 3.

SLIN Overview

Display   Change

Messages for Field Attributes(Warnings)

Program: ZAG_EXTENDED_CHECK Row: 11
Internal table LT_SFLIGHT[] is not addressed statically in the program
Can be suppressed using pragma ##NEEDED (or pseudo comment "#EC NEEDED)

Program: ZAG_EXTENDED_CHECK Row: 11
LT_SFLIGHT stands for 2 fields, for internal Table LT_SFLIGHT[], and for the table header line
Field string LT_SFLIGHT is not referenced statically in the program
Can be suppressed using pragma ##NEEDED (or pseudo comment "#EC NEEDED)

⌃ *Figure 3* Details of the Individual Check

Navigate to the related source code line by positioning the cursor on the message and clicking on either the Display or Change buttons on the toolbar. You can then correct the statement and go back to the results screen.

Sometimes it may not be possible to correct all results of the Extended Program Check. If you insist on writing the code in a way that the Extended Program Check doesn't like, you can suppress the check for this specific statement by adding a pseudo comment, which is suggested with the extended check result as shown in Figure 3.

For example, in the following source code, Extended Program Check displays an error message suggesting the use of the text element only for the first line.

```
MOVE 'Status1' TO lv_status1.
MOVE 'Status2' TO lv_status2. "#EC NOTEXT
```

The error message for the second line is suppressed with the pseudo comment `#EC NOTEXT`.

Note that the Extended Program Check utility checks the program only for static errors; it doesn't catch possible runtime errors.

Checking ABAP Programs for Naming Conventions with the Code Inspector

You can use the Code Inspector to check your development objects to make sure they adhere to a company's naming conventions.

Readability of programs is very important—it makes it easier for other developers to understand the logic of a program when they're trying to modify the source code. If every developer had a different style of programming, other developers would find it very difficult to read the source code. Therefore, naming conventions are usually defined by a company so that developers follow a set of rules when naming objects and elements while developing an application. To check that all development objects adhere to the naming conventions set by a company, the ABAP Workbench contains a Code Inspector tool that allows you to check development objects in terms of several aspects such as syntax, performance, and naming conventions, which we'll teach you how to use.

✓ And Here's How ...

Create the following respective objects in Transaction SCI to check ABAP programs for adherence to naming conventions using the Code Inspector (see Figure 1):

- ▶ Object set
- ▶ Variant
- ▶ Inspection

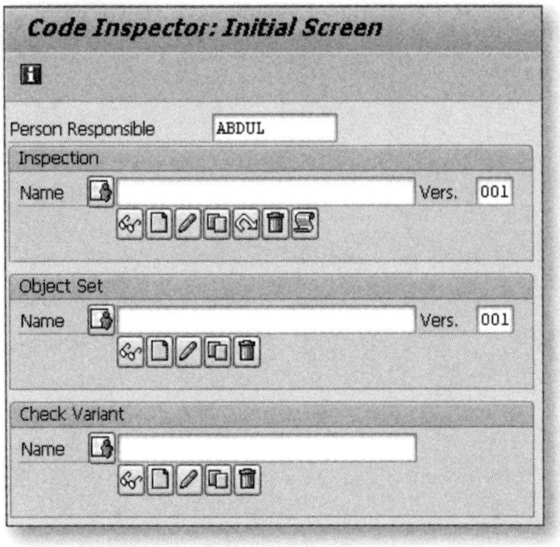

« **Figure 1** *Code Inspector Initial Screen*

First you'll create an object set, which is used to specify a set of objects that will be checked by the Code Inspector. Perform the following steps to create an object set:

1. Go to Transaction SCI.
2. Enter the name of the object set in the OBJECT SET section and click CREATE (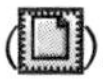).
3. You can use several selection options to build the object set. For example, enter the name of the ABAP program as shown in Figure 2 to restrict the object set to a single ABAP program.

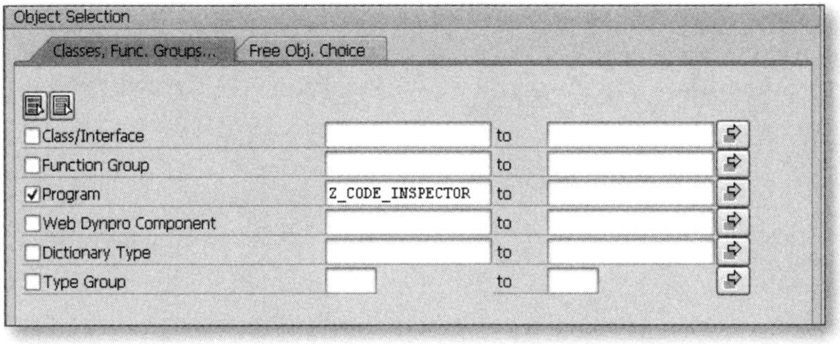

Figure 2 *Restricting the Object Set to a Single ABAP Program*

You can now save the object set and start creating the variant. Perform the following steps to create a variant:

1. Go to Transaction SCI.
2. Enter the name of the variant in the CHECK VARIANT section and click CREATE (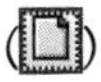).

3. Select the following tests from the list as shown in Figure 3 by clicking the respective checkboxes:

   ▶ NAMING CONVENTIONS

   ▶ ENHANCED NAMING CONVENTIONS FOR PROGRAMS

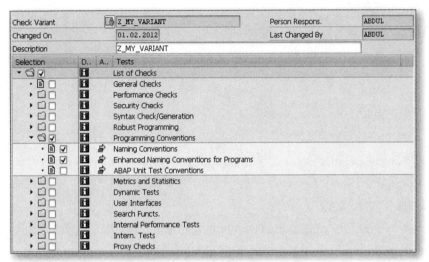

Check Variant			Z_MY_VARIANT	Person Respons.	ABDUL
Changed On			01.02.2012	Last Changed By	ABDUL
Description			Z_MY_VARIANT		
Selection	D..	A..	Tests		
▼ ☑	🛈		List of Checks		
· 📄 ☐	🛈		General Checks		
▶ ☐ ☐	🛈		Performance Checks		
▶ ☐ ☐	🛈		Security Checks		
▶ ☐ ☐	🛈		Syntax Check/Generation		
▶ ☐ ☐	🛈		Robust Programming		
▼ ☑	🛈		Programming Conventions		
· 📄 ☑	🛈	➡	Naming Conventions		
· 📄 ☑	🛈	➡	Enhanced Naming Conventions for Programs		
· 📄 ☐	🛈	➡	ABAP Unit Test Conventions		
▶ ☐ ☐	🛈		Metrics and Statistics		
▶ ☐ ☐	🛈		Dynamic Tests		
▶ ☐ ☐	🛈		User Interfaces		
▶ ☐ ☐	🛈		Search Functs.		
▶ ☐ ☐	🛈		Internal Performance Tests		
▶ ☐ ☐	🛈		Intern. Tests		
▶ ☐ ☐	🛈		Proxy Checks		

⊼ *Figure 3 Selecting the Appropriate Tests to Create a Variant to Check Naming Conventions*

4. To view and customize the rules that are defined to check naming conventions, click on the ➡ buttons.

You can now save the variant and start creating the inspection. Perform the following steps to create an inspection:

1. Go to Transaction SCI.

2. Enter the name of the inspection in the INSPECTION section and click CREATE (📋).

3. Select the object set and variant that you created in the previous steps.

4. Save the inspection.

You can now run the inspection to test the program that you selected in the object set according to the naming conventions defined in the variant. While you're in the INSPECTION screen, execute the inspection using the 🕒 button and check the results using the 🖾 button. The results will appear similar to Figure 4.

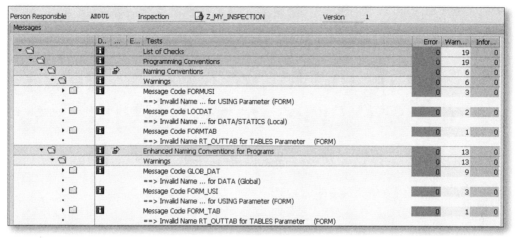

		D..	...	E...	Tests	Error	Warn...	Infor...
Person Responsible	ABDUL			Inspection	Z_MY_INSPECTION	Version	1	
Messages								
▼		ℹ			List of Checks	0	19	0
▼		ℹ			Programming Conventions	0	19	0
▼		ℹ			Naming Conventions	0	6	0
▼		ℹ			Warnings	0	6	0
▶		ℹ			Message Code FORMUSI	0	3	0
					==> Invalid Name ... for USING Parameter (FORM)			
▶		ℹ			Message Code LOCDAT	0	2	0
					==> Invalid Name ... for DATA/STATICS (Local)			
▶		ℹ			Message Code FORMTAB	0	1	0
					==> Invalid Name RT_OUTTAB for TABLES Parameter (FORM)			
▼		ℹ			Enhanced Naming Conventions for Programs	0	13	0
▼		ℹ			Warnings	0	13	0
▶		ℹ			Message Code GLOB_DAT	0	9	0
					==> Invalid Name ... for DATA (Global)			
▶		ℹ			Message Code FORM_USI	0	3	0
					==> Invalid Name ... for USING Parameter (FORM)			
▶		ℹ			Message Code FORM_TAB	0	1	0
					==> Invalid Name RT_OUTTAB for TABLES Parameter (FORM)			

≪   *Figure 4* *Inspection Results for Naming Conventions Tests*

You can also use several different tests to check ABAP programs as shown in Figure 3. Select the checkbox of each test that you want to run.

Using Code Inspector is an easy way to check the programs in your system to ensure the quality of the system. For example, you can configure the system to run the Code Inspector while releasing a transport request. Then, if there are resulting messages from the Code Inspector, the user has the option to review the messages or release the request despite error messages.

Tip 53

Testing and Improving the Quality of ABAP Programs with Unit Tests

You can use unit tests to test and improve the quality of ABAP programs.

Unit testing is an important part of the software development process because it helps you increase the quality of ABAP programs, especially in the agile software development area. You can take advantage of several benefits of using unit testing in the software development process. You can, for example, use unit tests to see if there is any problem after changing the program. It also helps you find the problems early while you're still developing the program.

Developers usually mix test codes into the original source code or write small test programs to test some portion of the source code. This will make the source code more complicated and difficult to maintain. To solve this problem, you can use the ABAP Unit tool to test your ABAP programs by separating the program into individual parts and testing each part separately to check if the part is running correctly.

✓ And Here's How ...

Let's follow an example to see how unit tests are run in the ABAP Workbench. Suppose that you're developing a subroutine to calculate the tax according to the price of a material, and you want to test this subroutine after changing the calculation logic. You can write the following test class at the end of the program to perform the desired test:

```
CLASS test DEFINITION FOR TESTING RISK LEVEL HARMLESS DURATION SHORT.
  PRIVATE SECTION.
```

```
      METHODS test_calculate_tax FOR TESTING.
ENDCLASS.
CLASS test IMPLEMENTATION.
  METHOD test_calculate_tax.
    DATA: price TYPE p VALUE 100,
          tax TYPE p.
    PERFORM calculate_tax USING price CHANGING tax.
    cl_aunit_assert=>assert_equals(
      act = tax
      exp = 18
      msg = 'Tax is calculated wrong!').
  ENDMETHOD.
ENDCLASS.
```

You can add more test classes and more methods into these classes according to the requirements. Then, you can run tests by calling the following menu path while you're in the ABAP Editor:

PROGRAM • TEST • UNIT TEST

You'll see a status message if the tests run successfully. If there are errors, the result is displayed as shown in Figure 1.

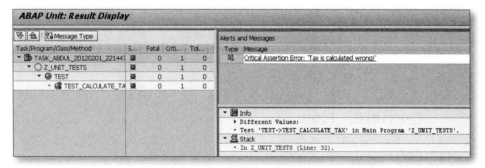

⩘ *Figure 1* The Result of the Unit Test When There's an Error

You may be wondering why you should write extra code to test the program. You can develop a program without unit tests, but when the requirements get more complex and the program logic starts to change many times, simple mistakes in the program may generate very big problems that aren't easy to find. You can easily analyze the problems and find which portion of the source code is the culprit if you implement test classes in ABAP programs.

Using the ABAP Runtime Analysis to Measure the Performance of an ABAP Program

You can use the ABAP Runtime Analysis tool while working on an ABAP program to measure its performance and avoid system problems later on.

Developers don't usually analyze the performance of ABAP programs unless there's a problem reported by end users or system administrators. However, sometimes you may not notice the negative performance impacts of some programs immediately, but they'll lead to poor system performance when these programs are connected. Then you have to go back, analyze, and correct all of these programs to increase your system performance. To avoid this problem, you can use the ABAP Runtime Analysis tool to analyze the performance of the program while developing the ABAP application.

✔ And Here's How ...

Access the ABAP Runtime Analysis tool using Transaction SAT (this is a new and improved version of Transaction SE30, which is used prior to SAP NetWeaver 7.0 EHP2). Figure 1 shows the initial screen of the ABAP Runtime Analysis tool.

The MEASR. tab allows you to create variants and run analysis with different options. You can analyze the measurement results in the EVALUATE tab.

Define measurement conditions and restrictions by creating a variant, or use the default variant proposed by the system. We'll use the default variant as an example, but you must restrict the conditions, especially if you're measuring the performance of long-running programs.

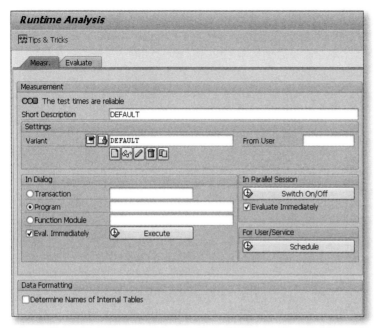

⌃ **Figure 1** ABAP Runtime Analysis Tool Initial Screen

You can measure the performance of the following object types using the ABAP Runtime Analysis tool:

▶ Transactions

▶ Programs

▶ Function modules

For example, select the PROGRAM radio button and enter the program name as "DEMO_SELECT_CURSOR". Then click the EXECUTE button to start the measurement process.

The program is started because you run it directly. When you exit the program, the measurement results are shown immediately in the following tabs on the result screen (a sample desktop configuration is shown in Figure 2):

▶ DESKTOP 1
 Similar to the new ABAP Debugger desktops, you can add any of the tools on the screen and adjust the position of tools according to your preference.

▶ HIT LIST
 Displays all measured statements and running times.

▶ DB TABLES

Displays all tables accessed during the trace. You can also see the measurements of the database access and buffering modes for each table.

▶ PROFL.

Displays the measurements results in a hierarchy grouped logically.

▶ TIMES

Displays more specific time values than the values displayed in the HIT LIST tab.

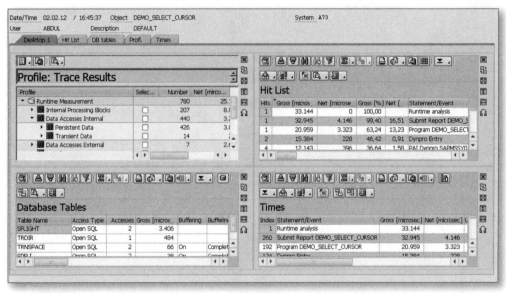

⌃ *Figure 2* *Customized Desktop to Display Four Tools in a Single View*

Several measures are given in the results. You can use the tools that are separated into tabs to analyze the performance of the ABAP program and to modify the program according to these results. You must make sure that the program is running without errors before running the program in the ABAP Runtime Analysis tool. If you run the program for the first time in the ABAP Runtime Analysis tool without running it directly, you may get incorrect results because the buffers and caches may be empty. After you run the program directly a few times, you'll get more accurate results in the ABAP Runtime Analysis tool.

Using Checkpoint Groups to Activate and Deactivate Checkpoints

You can use checkpoint groups to manage the activation settings of Break-Point, Log-Point, *and* Assert *statements in a production system.*

There are three types of checkpoint statements in ABAP: Break-Point, Log-Point, and Assert. You can use these statements to control, analyze, and test the flow of your ABAP programs. However, using these statements in a production system can be very dangerous because they can create a massive amount of unnecessary logs or break the execution of the running program unexpectedly. To avoid this risk, checkpoint groups give you the option to analyze the ABAP program by activating Break-Point, Log-Point, and Assert statements only when you need them and deactivating them after you finish your analysis.

✅ And Here's How ...

You can create and maintain checkpoint groups in Transaction SAAB. To create a checkpoint group, enter the name and click CREATE (🗋). In the popup dialog that opens, enter the description and click CONTINUE (✔). You can now save the checkpoint group and use it in the checkpoint statements as shown in the following examples:

```
LOG-POINT ID ZTEST FIELDS lv_test.
BREAK-POINT ID ZTEST.
ASSERT ID ZTEST CONDITION lv_test EQ 'X'.
```

Checkpoint groups are linked to the `Break-Point`, `Log-Point`, and `Assert` statements by adding an `ID` statement as shown in the preceding example. Note that if you don't link `Break-Point` or `Assert` statements with a checkpoint group, they'll always be active. However, `Log-Point` statements must always be linked to the checkpoint groups.

To activate the checkpoint, go to Transaction SAAB and open the checkpoint group in change mode by entering the checkpoint group name and clicking the CHANGE (🖉) button. Navigate to the ACTIVATION tab as shown in Figure 1.

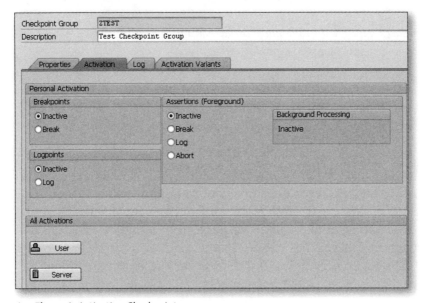

⌃ **Figure 1** Activating Checkpoints

The following modes are possible for checkpoints:

► BREAKPOINTS

  ► INACTIVE: Breakpoint is inactive.

  ► BREAK: Breakpoint is active.

► LOGPOINTS

  ► INACTIVE: Logpoint is inactive.

  ► LOG: Logpoint is active.

▶ ASSERTIONS

  ▶ INACTIVE: Assertion is inactive.

  ▶ BREAK: When assertion statement is reached, it behaves like a breakpoint.

  ▶ LOG: When assertion statement is reached, it behaves like a logpoint.

  ▶ ABORT: Program terminates with runtime error.

When you select the `Break` condition for `Assert` statements, a popup triggers as shown in Figure 2. Because the program can't stop in the debugger when it's running in the background, you must specify what the system should do in this case. You can select either abort the program or treat the current `Assert` statement as a `Log-Point` statement.

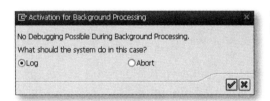

《 Figure 2 *Activate Assertions for Background Processing*

After selecting the operation modes, you have the following options to activate the checkpoint group:

▶ ACTIVATION FOR INDIVIDUAL USERS
  You can activate the checkpoints for individual users using the USER button.

▶ ACTIVATION FOR INDIVIDUAL SERVERS
  You can activate the checkpoints for individual application servers using the SERVER button.

You can activate the checkpoint either for a single user or for all users on a single application server. These settings help you use the checkpoints without interrupting the other users using the same SAP system.

Now you can run the ABAP program that has checkpoints in the source. The behavior of the checkpoints will be determined by settings that you have defined in the checkpoint group. If you use the `Log-Point` statement or `Assertion` statement in log mode, you can open the checkpoint group, navigate to the LOG tab, and analyze the log entries that you've created in the ABAP program using the `Log-Point` statement as shown in Figure 3.

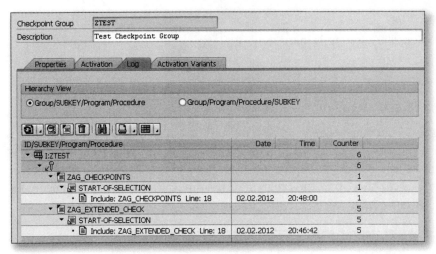

⌃ *Figure 3 Analyzing Logs Created by the Log-Point Statement*

Be careful when activating the logpoints. If you leave the logpoints active for a long time, system performance may be affected due to uncontrolled growth in the database tables. Make sure to deactivate the checkpoint groups after you've finished analyzing the program as well.

Tip 56

Analyzing the Memory Consumption of ABAP Programs

You can find the causes of memory-related problems by analyzing memory snapshots captured via different methods.

When you're developing an ABAP program, it can have memory problems due to several reasons. You may want to investigate the memory consumption of the program due to the poor performance at different times to better understand the reasons for the performance problems. You can create memory snapshots using different tools, depending on what you're doing at the time, and then analyze and compare the memory consumption of the program in the Memory Inspector tool.

✓ And Here's How ...

Memory snapshots contain the information about the memory usage of the program at a particular time. They can be created in three ways. The easiest way is using the following menu path:

> SYSTEM • UTILITIES • MEMORY ANALYSIS • CREATE MEMORY SNAPSHOT

There is also the Memory Analysis tool in the ABAP Debugger that helps you create memory snapshots directly from the ABAP Debugger. If you're using the Memory Analysis tool in the ABAP Debugger, you can also create memory snapshots from the SERVICES menu of the tool by choosing:

> SERVICES • TOOL-SPECIFIC • CREATE MEMORY SNAPSHOT

If you want to create a memory snapshot for programs running in the background, you can't use the prior two options. Use the following method to create a memory snapshot at any point in the ABAP program:

```
CALL METHOD
  cl_abap_memory_utilities=>write_memory_consumption_file
```

Be careful when using this method because it can create too many files on the server if you use it in the loops running too many times.

Analysis

After you create the snapshots, go to Transaction S_MEMORY_INSPECTOR to analyze them. You'll see a list of the snapshot files created on the server as shown in Figure 1.

❯ *Figure 1 Snapshot Files Created on the Server*

Double-click on any of the files to analyze the memory consumption saved on the file. Figure 2 shows an example view of the memory snapshot.

❯ *Figure 2 Analyzing Memory Snapshots*

You can use the tools listed in the left MEMORY SNAPSHOT / VIEW tree to perform detailed analysis on the snapshot.

If you want to compare the currently open snapshot with another, double-click on another snapshot. The system will open the second snapshot and show two snapshots assigned to labels t_0 and t_1 with yellow and blue icons. Click the t_0 and t_1 buttons on the toolbar to display each snapshot's details. There is also a t_1 – t_0 button on the toolbar—this displays the different values for the memory consumption. Figure 3 displays the labels, buttons, and icons assigned to the snapshot files.

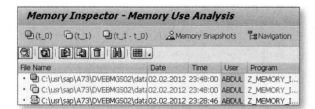

« Figure 3 Opening Two Snapshots Together to Compare in the Memory Inspector

If you click on the DISPLAY DIFFERENCE button (t_1 - t_0), it will show the difference values for the memory consumption in the tool area as shown in Figure 4.

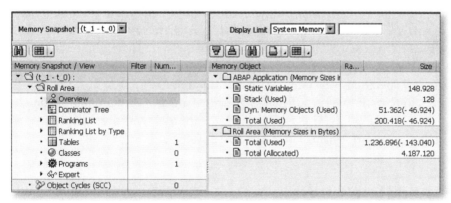

⌃ Figure 4 Displaying the Difference for the Memory Consumption Values between Two Snapshot Files

On the left side, only the objects that have different memory consumptions are displayed. On the right side, the different values for the memory consumptions are listed. You can perform a detailed analysis on the memory consumption of the program using this tool to help you find which objects are consuming more memory and how the memory consumptions are changed at different times. You can improve the memory consumptions and hence the quality of the ABAP programs using this technique.

Tip 57

Analyzing Database Accesses in ABAP Programs Using the Performance Trace Tool

You can use the Performance Trace tool to trace the performance of the SQL statements in an ABAP program and minimize performance problems.

When you write an ABAP program, you usually use Open SQL to write SQL statements that are independent of the underlying database system. The SAP system converts the Open SQL statements to embedded SQL and passes these statements to the database. In most cases, performance problems in ABAP programs are caused by database operations. To eliminate, or at least minimize these performance problems, it's important to write efficient SQL statements in ABAP programs. You can use the SQL Trace utility in the Performance Trace tool to analyze the SQL statements and their performance on the database system.

✓ And Here's How ...

Access the Performance Trace tool via Transaction ST05. You can trace five different options in the Performance Trace tool as shown in the SELECT TRACE section in Figure 1.

Select the SQL TRACE checkbox and click the ACTIVATE TRACE button on the toolbar to activate tracing for database accesses. You can also activate tracing with a filter using the ACTIVATE TRACE WITH FILTER button. You can filter SQL traces according to the following information:

- ▶ Username
- ▶ Transaction name
- ▶ Program name
- ▶ Process number
- ▶ Table name (include or exclude)

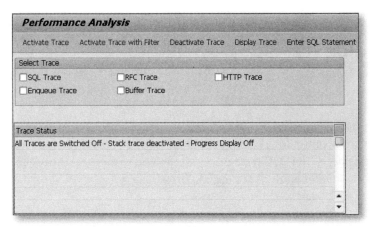

⌃ **Figure 1** *Performance Trace Initial Screen*

When you activate the SQL Trace utility, the TRACE STATUS text area is updated as shown in Figure 2. All database activities are logged in the trace file until you deactivate the trace.

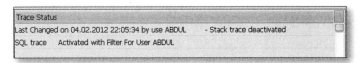

⌃ **Figure 2** *Updated Trace Status*

When you finish running the program, deactivate the trace using the DEACTIVATE TRACE button. Display the recorded data using the DISPLAY TRACE button. You'll see a selection screen where you can filter the trace results. After you run the report by clicking EXECUTE (), the results are displayed as shown in Figure 3.

Trace List

DDIC Information   Explain

HH:MM:SS.MS	ΣDurtn	Program Name	Obj. Name	Operation	Curs	Array	ΣRecs.	RC	Conn	Statement
22:15:58.645	1.033	BCALV_FULLSCREEN_DEMO	SFLIGHT	OPEN	2352	0	0	0	R/3	SELECT WHERE "MANDT" = '001'
22:15:58.646	103	BCALV_FULLSCREEN_DEMO	SFLIGHT	FETCH	2352	142	30	0	R/3	
22:15:58.661	10	SAPLSDIFRUNTIME	DDFTX	PREPARE	0	0	0	0	R/3	SELECT WHERE "TABNAME" = ? AND "DDLANGUAGE"
22:15:58.662	655	SAPLSDIFRUNTIME	DDFTX	OPEN	2352	0	0	0	R/3	SELECT WHERE "TABNAME" = 'SFLIGHT' AND "DDLAN
22:15:58.662	97	SAPLSDIFRUNTIME	DDFTX	FETCH	2352	51	15	0	R/3	
22:15:58.668	11	SAPLSKBS	V_LTDX	PREPARE	0	0	0	0	R/3	SELECT WHERE "MANDT" = ? AND "RELID" = ? AND "F
22:15:58.668	628	SAPLSKBS	V_LTDX	OPEN	2352	0	0	0	R/3	SELECT WHERE "MANDT" = '001' AND "RELID" = 'LT'
22:15:58.669	19	SAPLSKBS	V_LTDX	FETCH	2352	91	0	0	R/3	
22:15:58.670	9	SAPLSDIFRUNTIME	DDFTX	PREPARE	0	0	0	0	R/3	SELECT WHERE "TABNAME" = ? AND "DDLANGUAGE"
22:15:58.670	463	SAPLSDIFRUNTIME	DDFTX	OPEN	2352	0	0	0	R/3	SELECT WHERE "TABNAME" = 'SFLIGHT' AND "DDLAN

⌃ *Figure 3 The Extended Trace List*

The extended trace list is displayed by default. You can see all executed SQL statements and the execution values for each statement. Notice that there is more than one line for each statement. The SQL Trace utility allows you to measure the execution times of the following operations for each SQL statement:

▶ DECLARE
Declares a cursor for an SQL statement.

▶ PREPARE
Converts the SQL statement.

▶ OPEN
Opens a cursor.

▶ FETCH
Passes the records from the database to the SAP system.

▶ REOPEN
Opens the cursor again that has been prepared for a SELECT statement.

▶ EXEC
Executes the statement that performs a change in the database.

▶ REEXEC
Opens the cursor again that has been prepared for an EXEC statement.

The extended trace list usually gives you more detail than you need.

If you want to see the aggregated results according to the SQL statements, choose TRACE LIST • SUMMARIZE TRACE BY SQL STATEMENT.

This list allows you to overview the execution times according to the SQL statements. You can also aggregate the trace list by table access by clicking TRACE LIST • COMBINED TABLE ACCESSES.

You can access the technical information for the tables by selecting the relevant row and clicking the DDIC INFORMATION button on the toolbar. You can also jump to the index and table fields from this screen.

Another useful function that is available on the toolbar is EXPLAIN, which displays more information about the SQL statements depending on the installed database system. For example, you can analyze which indexes are used while accessing the database using this function.

As you can see, you can use SQL Trace to analyze several types of information regarding database accesses. When you're tracing database access, make sure that you have used the proper filters; otherwise, it will be difficult to perform an analysis on a huge number of trace records. You should also deactivate the trace as soon as you're finished because it generates too much information, which may reduce system performance.

Finding the Right Event to Trigger a Workflow

You can find the most suitable event to trigger your workflow by using the Event Trace tool.

When you're developing a workflow in SAP Business Workflow, one of the more difficult tasks is finding a suitable event to configure to trigger the workflow. These events help you trigger workflows to run specific tasks after certain conditions. Although many events exist in the standard transactions, it may not be easy to find the list of these events. You can use the Event Trace tool to record all events that are triggered after a specific task and then find and use the most suitable one to trigger your workflow.

✓ And Here's How ...

The Event Trace tool allows you to record all events triggered after a specific task in a business transaction. We'll show you an example to see how the Event Trace tool can be used to find an event.

Suppose that you want to find all events triggered after you change a sales order in Transaction VA02. You must activate the Event Trace tool and simulate the process to see the list of events. Follow these steps:

1. Open a sales order in Transaction VA02.
2. Go to Transaction SWELS in another session to switch on the Event Trace tool. You can also use the following menu path on the SAP Easy Access menu:

> TOOLS • BUSINESS WORKFLOW • DEVELOPMENT • UTILITIES • EVENTS • EVENT TRACE
> • SWITCH EVENT TRACE ON/OFF

A popup dialog opens as shown in Figure 1.

« Figure 1 *Switching the Event Trace Tool On*

3. Click the SWITCH ON button to start logging the events.

4. Now a new RESTRICTIONS FOR TRACE button appears near the SWITCH ON button. You can use this button to restrict the conditions of the events. This function is useful especially when many users are logged on to the system and running different transactions. Otherwise, it would be difficult to distinguish between the events triggered from different transactions by different users. When you click this button, a popup opens as shown in Figure 2.

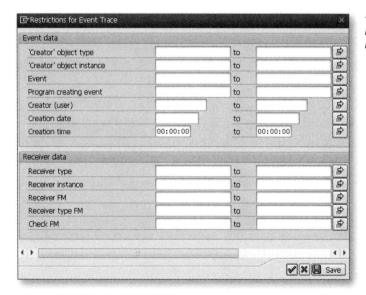

« Figure 2 *Restrictions for Event Trace*

5. Maintain the fields on the selection screen to restrict the events to be traced.

6. Go to Transaction VA02 to change any information in the sales order to trigger the change event.

7. Save the sales order, and then go back to Transaction SWELS to switch off the trace by clicking the SWITCH OFF button on the popup window.

8. Now you can analyze the trace records. Go to Transaction SWEL, or use the following menu path on the SAP Easy Access menu:

> TOOLS • BUSINESS WORKFLOW • DEVELOPMENT • UTILITIES • EVENTS • EVENT TRACE • SWITCH EVENT TRACE ON/OFF

9. Select the appropriate options on the selection screen to filter the trace records. After running the report, the results will be displayed as shown in Figure 3.

> **Figure 3** Displaying Event Trace Records

As shown in Figure 3, when you change the sales order CHANGED event, the BUS2032 object is triggered. This means you can use this event to trigger the workflow that must be run after sales order changes.

There are several events triggered after specific tasks hidden in the SAP transactions. This tool can help you find the correct event when you want to create a workflow that will be run after a specific condition. There can even be more than one event running in some conditions. In such cases, you need to trace the program by running it with different parameter values to find the right event.

Tip 59

Using the Work Item Selection Tool to Analyze Workflow Logs

You can display and analyze executed work items when you're having workflow issues with the Work Item Selection tool.

SAP Business Workflow is great for developing complex business processes in the SAP system—you have the ability to combine several tasks in a single workflow and configure it to run each task by different users or as a background process. However, when the workflow isn't running as expected or doesn't run at all, it can be very difficult to find the problem. In this tip, we'll show you how you can use the Work Item Selection tool to find workflow problems by displaying and analyzing the logs generated by the workflow process.

And Here's How ...

Business workflows usually contain several work items running sequentially or parallel and each by different users. The Work Item Selection tool displays the detailed execution information for each work item if it isn't explicitly hidden from the log. In this tool, you can find the workflow that doesn't run or produces unexpected results and see the task statuses, the values of container variables, agent information, and so on that will help you solve the problem.

To access and use the tool to find workflow problems, follow these steps:

1. Access the Work Item Selection tool with Transaction SWI1, or use the following menu path:

> TOOLS • BUSINESS WORKFLOW • DEVELOPMENT • UTILITIES • WORK ITEM SELECTION

2. Select the appropriate values in the selection screen for your purpose. The results are displayed in an ALV grid list as shown in Figure 1.

ID	Work Item Type	Language	Work item text
8607...	Dialog Step	Turkish	Generic decision task
8607...	(Sub)workflow	Turkish	Sales Order
8607...	Background Step	English	Sipariş 12094 reddedildi.
8607...	Background Step	English	SALESORDERRJ
8607...	Dialog Step	English	12094 mumaralı satınalma siparişi ABDUL tarafından yaratıldı.
8607...	(Sub)workflow	English	Sales Order
8607...	Background Step	English	Sipariş 12093 Onaylandı
8607...	Background Step	English	SALESORDERAP
8607...	Dialog Step	English	12093 mumaralı satınalma siparişi ABDUL tarafından yaratıldı.
8607...	(Sub)workflow	English	Sales Order

⌃ *Figure 1 Displaying Work Items*

In addition to the standard ALV functions, the following functions are available on the toolbar:

▶ EXECUTE WORK ITEM (⟠)
Select a work item from the list and click this button to execute the selected work item.

▶ DISPLAY WORK ITEM (⟠)
Use this function to display the work item details.

▶ DISPLAY WORKFLOW LOG (⟠)
Use this function to overview the logs and statuses of the workflow steps as shown in Figure 2. This is one of the most useful functions in the Work Item Selection tool.

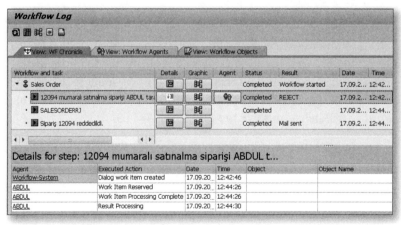

⌃ *Figure 2 Displaying the Workflow Log*

The following functions are available for each workflow step:

▶ The DETAILS button (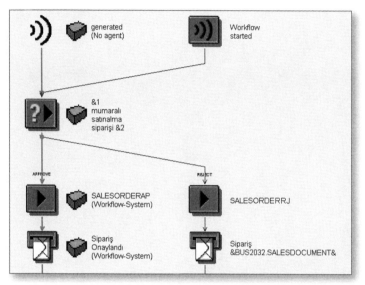 placeholder) allows you to overview the execution details of the work items.

▶ The AGENT button allows you to display the users involved in the workflow.

▶ The GRAPHIC button displays the workflow and the execution path as shown in Figure 3.

≫ **Figure 3** *Displaying the Execution Path of the Workflow*

▶ DISPLAY WORK ITEM CONTAINER
Use this function to display the values of the container elements when the step is executed.

▶ DISPLAY TASK
Use this function to navigate directly to the workflow task to check the technical details.

There are many more functions that you can use to analyze the workflow logs. When you're using SAP Business Workflow to execute your business processes, Work Item Selection is a must-use tool that helps system administrators and workflow developers analyze all kinds of details in the workflow runtime.

Part 7

ABAP Data Dictionary

Things You'll Learn in this Section

The ABAP Data Dictionary is a central point for managing data and data definitions in SAP systems. Tables, views, and other dictionary objects are defined in the ABAP Data Dictionary independently of the underlying database product. There are several tools in the ABAP Data Dictionary to help you create dictionary objects. This part of the book provides tips and tricks to help you streamline the process of creating and managing dictionary objects and data definitions. You'll also learn practical ways to create user interfaces on top of these objects, such as maintenance screens and search helps.

Tip 60

Configuring Display and Maintenance Options for Database Tables

You can configure the display and maintenance options of a table to restrict the use of the Data Browser and Maintain Table Views tools.

Normally, you can display or maintain the records of database tables in the Data Browser tool (Transaction SE16) or in the Maintain Table Views (Transaction SM30 and SM31) tool. You can configure display and maintenance options for both tables and views in their relevant editors.[1] This setting is overlooked most of the time and only used if the table view maintenance will be generated. However, it has some extra functionality that can be used when you want to set restrictions on creating maintenance dialogs and displaying or maintaining the records of a table.

✅ And Here's How ...

The Data Browser tool can be used directly for maintenance, but you must create the Table Maintenance screen to maintain the records of a table via the Maintain Table View tool. You can restrict the use of these tools for tables and views using the DISPLAY and MAINTENANCE options.

When you create a database table, access the DATA BROWSER/TABLE VIEW MAINT. combo box in the DELIVERY AND MAINTENANCE tab as shown in Figure 1. Here you can configure the delivery and maintain options for a table.

---

1 This isn't available for help views; they aren't relevant to these tools and aren't used in search helps.

《 Figure 1 *Delivery and Maintenance Options for a Database Table*

You can choose from one of the following three options:

▶ DISPLAY/MAINTENANCE NOT ALLOWED
The table or view can't be displayed or maintained using standard tools. This option can be used to restrict the display options for tables and views that contain secure data. You can't even generate a maintenance dialog for these types of tables/views. Even if you've created the maintenance dialog before setting this field, you can't open the maintenance dialog after setting this value.

▶ DISPLAY/MAINTENANCE ALLOWED
The table or view can be displayed using the Data Browser or Maintain Table Views tools.

▶ DISPLAY/MAINTENANCE ALLOWED WITH RESTRICTIONS
The table contents can be displayed via the Data Browser, but you can't maintain the table directly using the Maintain Table Views tool. However, you can generate the table maintenance screen and include it in view clusters or call in ABAP programs using the function module `View_Maintenance_Call`.

You can also use the same options for database views. When you're creating or modifying a database view, you can open the MAINT.STATUS tab and configure the delivery and maintenance options as shown in Figure 2.

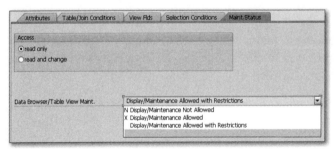

《 Figure 2 *Delivery and Maintenance Options for a View*

Note that the DISPLAY/MAINTENANCE NOT ALLOWED option isn't available for maintenance views—it would be meaningless to create a maintenance view but not allow users to use it.

Generating Table Maintenance Dialogs for Database Tables or Views

You can use the Generate Table Maintenance Dialog tool to create standardized maintenance dialogs and allow end users to maintain tables and views.

You can maintain the customizing tables in SAP systems according to specific business requirements using table maintenance dialogs without the need of any ABAP development. Table maintenance dialogs help you create or modify the records of tables/views and transport changed data using transport management. In this tip, we'll show you how you can create table maintenance dialogs for any tables/views that you want to be maintained by end users.

✓ And Here's How ...

The Table Maintenance Generator tool is used to create table maintenance dialogs and can be accessed with Transactions SE54 or SE11. This tool can be used only if the display and maintenance options of a table/view are set properly. You can't create table maintenance dialogs for tables/views if the display and maintenance options are set to DISPLAY/MAINTENANCE NOT ALLOWED.

Perform the following steps to create a table maintenance dialog for a database table:

1. Open the table in Transaction SE11.

2. Start the Table Maintenance Generator by choosing UTILITIES • TABLE MAINTENANCE GENERATOR. Figure 1 shows the initial screen of the Table Maintenance Generator tool.

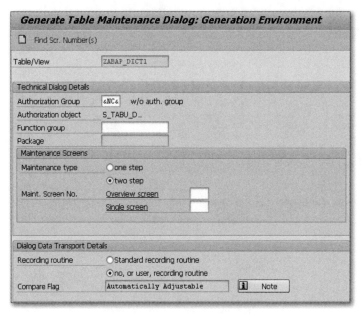

⤴ *Figure 1 Table Maintenance Generator Initial Screen*

3. Assign an authorization group to the table maintenance dialog to restrict the maintenance of the table/view using authorization object S_TABU_DIS. You can create different profiles for different objects using this authorization object.

4. Specify the name of the function group for the function modules that will be created.

5. Select the maintenance type:

   ▶ If you select ONE STEP, only one screen will be generated, and the records will be displayed and maintained on a table list.

   ▶ If you select TWO STEP, you can generate two screens: one for displaying the list and the other for displaying or maintaining a single record.

6. Define the screen numbers for OVERVIEW SCREEN and SINGLE SCREEN that will be generated according to the maintenance type. If you selected ONE STEP as the maintenance type, you only need to provide the screen number for OVERVIEW

SCREEN. You can also use the FIND SCR. NUMBER(S) button to open the tool that will help you find the available screen number(s). The following three options are available to help you find the proper screen numbers:

- ► PROPOSE SCREEN NUMBER(S)
- ► DISPLAY FREE NUMBER RANGES
- ► LIST SCREEN NUMBERS

7. Specify the change recording type for the changes that will be made using this table maintenance dialog.

- ► STANDARD RECORDING ROUTINE
  The changes are recorded by the standard recording routine.

- ► NO, OR USER, RECORDING ROUTINE
  Changes aren't recorded by default. You can define your own event routines to handle the changes.

Click the CREATE button (⬚) to create the maintenance dialog. You can now test the dialog in Transaction SM30. Figure 2 shows an example of a one-step table maintenance dialog.

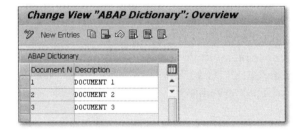

《 Figure 2 *One-Step Table Maintenance Dialog*

Alternatively, you can also create table maintenance dialogs in Transaction SE54. It will take you to the same screen as just described. The only difference is the initial screen. You must provide the table name, select the GENERATED OBJECTS option, and click the CREATE/CHANGE button to enter the maintenance screen.

You can now easily add, modify, or delete records from tables and views. End users will be able to maintain customizing data in the test system and transport it to the production system without any technical knowledge.

Tip (62)

Creating and Using Foreign Keys to Define Relationships between Database Tables

You can use foreign-key relationships in the ABAP Data Dictionary not only to perform value checks in screens, but also to create better relationships in different type views and lock objects.

In the relational database concept, a foreign key can be defined as a field or set of fields of a database table referenced to another table. Foreign keys are used to ensure the integrity of the data by allowing the creation of records only if the foreign key fields exist in the reference table. In this tip, we'll show you how to create and extend foreign keys in the ABAP Data Dictionary, which you'll use to create better relationships between dictionary objects.

✓ And Here's How ...

When you create a foreign key for a column, the value check is performed for input fields; you just make sure that the value in this column always exists in the check table.

Suppose that you want to create a database table to store the received order details. In the most primitive technique, you create a single table and put all details on that table. However, in relational database design, you create separate tables to avoid repeating the same information in more than one row of a table. For example, you can create another table to store customer details to avoid repeating the customer details. Figure 1 shows the sample database diagram for this example.

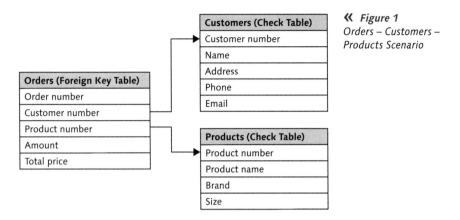

« Figure 1
*Orders – Customers –
Products Scenario*

As you can see in Figure 1, customers and products are stored in separate tables. The orders table contains only the keys of the customers and products. For example, if a customer places more than one order, only the customer number is used more than once in the table, and all customer details are stored in the customer table in a single row.

Now, suppose that you want to make sure that the values of the customer number and product number columns in the orders table also exist in the customers table and the products table; otherwise, the data will be inconsistent. You can create a foreign key for the CUSTOMER NUMBER and PRODUCT NUMBER fields in the orders table to avoid this inconsistency.

You can create a foreign key for a column while you're creating or modifying a table in Transaction SE11:

1. Select the field name from the list, and click the FOREIGN KEYS button (⬚) on the toolbar of the column list to start creating a foreign key. A popup window opens as shown in Figure 2; enter the details of the foreign key.

2. Enter the name of the table that will be used as a check table in the CHECK TABLE field, and click the GENERATE PROPOSAL button. The key fields of the check table are listed, and a proposal is generated as shown in Figure 2, according to the domains of the columns. Note that the check table must have the primary key field, which has the same domain as the column for which you're creating a foreign key. If there are key fields that you don't have in your foreign-key table, you can click the GENERIC checkbox for those fields or enter a constant value in the CONSTANT column.

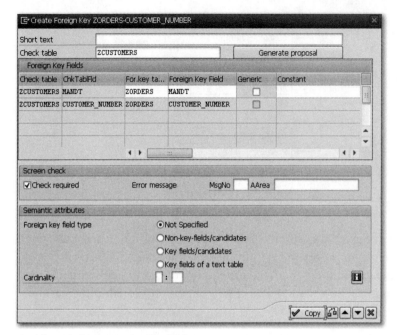

⌃ **Figure 2** *Create Foreign Key Dialog*

3. Select the CHECK REQUIRED checkbox to activate the value checks on the screens in which the foreign key field is used. You can also customize the error message that will be displayed when a user tries to enter a value in a foreign key field that doesn't exist in the check table. You can disable the value checks on the screens by unchecking the CHECK REQUIRED checkbox. You may need to disable the value checks for foreign keys that you're defining to create maintenance views, help views, or lock objects.

4. Define the cardinality and the type of the foreign key fields in the SEMANTIC ATTRIBUTES section. These settings don't affect the value checks on the screens. They are used only to define a foreign key to create maintenance views, help views, or lock objects. You can select one of the following three options for the FOREIGN KEY FIELD TYPE:

   ▸ NON-KEY-FIELDS/CANDIDATES
     In the foreign-key table, the foreign key fields are neither the primary keys of the table nor do they uniquely identify a record of the table.

   ▸ KEY FIELDS/CANDIDATES
     In the foreign-key table, the foreign key fields are either the primary keys of the table or uniquely identify a record of the table.

▶ KEY FIELDS OF A TEXT TABLE
This option is used to create text tables. The only difference between the foreign-key table and the check table is that there is an additional LANGUAGE KEY field in the check table. This type of table is used to create text descriptions in several languages.

The CARDINALITY option is used to define the number of records that can exist in the foreign key and check tables. On the left input box, you can choose from the following entries:

▶ 1: ENTRY IN THE CHECK FIELD MUST EXIST
For each record of the foreign-key table, there is exactly one record in the check table.

▶ C: ENTRY IN THE CHECK FIELD CAN EXIST
For each record of the foreign-key table, there may not be a record in the check table.

On the right input box, you can choose from the following entries:

▶ CN: EACH RECORD IN THE CHECK TABLE HAS ANY NUMBER OF DEPENDENT RECORDS
For each record of the check table, there can be any number of dependent records in the foreign-key table.

▶ C: EACH RECORD IN CHECK TABLE HAS A MAXIMUM OF ONE DEPENDENT RECORD
For each record of the check table, there can be at most one dependent record in the foreign-key table.

▶ N: EACH RECORD IN THE CHECK TABLE HAS AT LEAST ONE DEPENDENT RECORD
For each record of the check table, there is at least one dependent record in the foreign-key table.

▶ 1: EACH RECORD IN THE CHECK TABLE HAS EXACTLY ONE DEPENDENT RECORD
For each record of the check table, there is exactly one dependent record in the foreign-key table.

You can use any combinations to form the desired cardinality. For example, entering the combination "1:CN" ensures that for each record in the foreign-key table, there is always one record in the check table, but there can be many records in the foreign-key table for each record in the check table.

5. Check the definition using the CHECK button () on the popup toolbar, and click the COPY button to save the foreign-key definition if there are no errors in the check results.

Tip 63

Using Foreign-Key Relationships to Create Maintenance Views

You can create maintenance views to maintain logically linked database tables en masse.

In relational database design, several tables are created to form a single object. Each table represents a single entity of an object, and these tables are logically linked together using foreign-key relationships. This type of design has many technical advantages, but it becomes very difficult to maintain the data in these tables. There will be several database tables, and when you need to change the records in one of these tables, you need to take care of all related tables also to preserve the consistency. To solve this problem, the ABAP Data Dictionary allows you to create maintenance views using foreign-key relationships to maintain logically linked tables in a single view.

✓ And Here's How ...

When you create a view in Transaction SE11, choose the maintenance view from the listed view types to start creating a maintenance view. The CREATE VIEW screen will open as shown in Figure 1; start by entering the table names that you want to maintain in a single view.

Classic database views allow you to create join conditions manually, but a foreign-key relationship must exist with suitable cardinality between tables that will be used in the maintenance view. You can only enter the name of the primary table; all other tables must be selected from the foreign key fields by clicking the RELATIONSHIPS button. All tables that have foreign-key relationships with the main table are listed in a popup as shown in Figure 2.

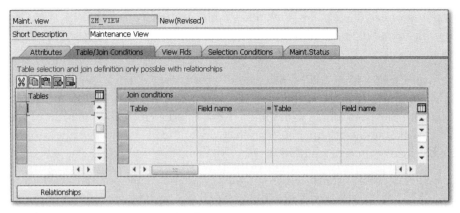

☆ *Figure 1* *Create Maintenance View Screen*

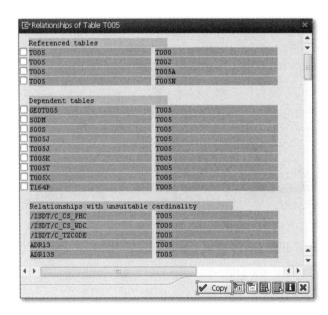

« *Figure 2* *Foreign-Key*
Relationship List for Table T005

You can select from either referenced or dependent tables. Tables that are linked with unsuitable cardinalities are also listed, but they can't be selected to transfer to the view. You must correct the cardinality if you want to use any of these tables in the maintenance view.

The following cardinality rules must be followed while creating a foreign key:

▶ If the secondary table is the check table, N:1 dependency already exists, and you can add this table into the view.

▶ If the secondary table is the foreign-key table, cardinality must be N:1 or N:C to be able to add the table into the view. That means there must be 0 or 1 records in the primary table for each record in the secondary tables.

When you finish adding tables, navigate to the VIEW FLDS tab to select the fields that you want to include in the view. Click the TABLE FIELDS button to open a popup with the list of all the tables in the view. Select a table, and the fields of the table are listed in the popup. You can select any of the fields and insert it into the view by clicking the COPY button.

All key fields of the primary table and all key fields of the secondary table that aren't linked to the primary table with a foreign key must be included in the view to make sure that the records are correctly inserted into the tables that are included in the view.

After adding the fields, you can modify their maintenance attributes just after the field name if you want to assign a special attribute to the field. Leave it empty if you don't want to add any restrictions. The following options are available:

▶ **R:**
The field is added as read only, and you can't modify the value of the field on the table maintenance screen

▶ **S:**
The field is used to create a subset of the table. The subset fields are displayed when you enter the table maintenance screen, and only the subset of the data is displayed for the maintenance.

▶ **H:**
The field isn't shown in the maintenance view.

You add selection conditions in the SELECTION CONDITIONS tab and specify the maintenance options in the MAINT.STATUS tab. Save and activate the view.

Finally, you can create table maintenance dialog using the procedure described in Tip 61.

Now you can maintain all of the tables that you included in the view on a single screen using Transaction SM30; you can even customize the screen by modifying the maintenance attributes. You can use this technique even for a single table to create customized maintenance screens. For example, you can make it read only, hide some fields, and allow users to modify only some of the fields.

Assigning Value Tables to Domains to Propose Foreign Keys for Database Fields

You can assign a value table property to a domain to propose this value as a foreign-key table, while creating a foreign key for a field that uses this domain.

Domains are used to define value ranges to the data elements in the ABAP Data Dictionary. To do this, you should link database fields and structure components with domains by using these data elements.

However, defining the value ranges directly in the domain may not be possible because of the customer requirement to be able to change the contents of the value table. In this tip, we'll show you how you can assign a value table to the domain that will be proposed as a check table when you create a foreign key for fields that use this domain.

✔ And Here's How ...

When you're defining a domain, you can modify the fixed values, intervals, and value table property in the VALUE RANGE tab as shown in Figure 1.

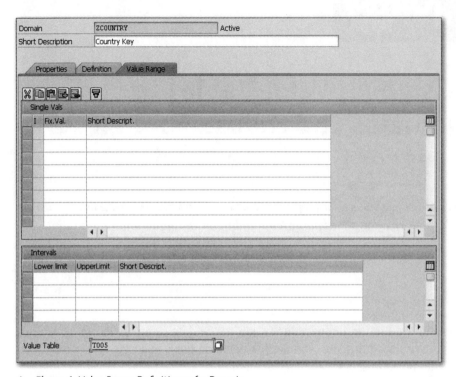

⤊ *Figure 1* *Value Range Definitions of a Domain*

In Figure 1, you can see the example definition of a domain ZCOUNTRY, which can be used in the database fields that will hold the country information. You can specify the country list in the SINGLE VALS table more easily, but it would be very difficult to update the country list in the future. Another option is to use the intervals, but that option isn't suitable for our case.

Alternatively, you can create the country list in another table and link to the database field by creating a foreign-key definition. This time, you have to remember the name of the country table whenever you use the data element that linked to this domain in a new field. To solve this problem, you can add the name of the table in the VALUE TABLE field on the domain definition as shown in Figure 1.

However, adding the table name in the VALUE TABLE field isn't enough to perform a value check in screens. When you create a foreign-key relationship for the database field or structure component that linked to this domain, it helps you by proposing a table name, as shown in Figure 2.

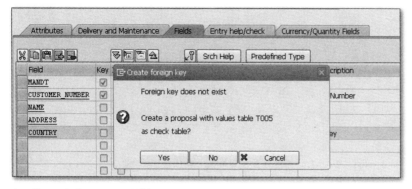

⌃ *Figure 2* *Proposing a Table Name*

Create the foreign key by clicking YES and continuing to specify the details of the foreign key.

Tip **65**

Adjusting Screen Elements with Conversion Routines

You can create conversion routines to automatically adjust screen fields and formatting.

You may need to perform a format conversion on a screen field before inserting the field value into the database or before displaying a database field on a screen. This is especially needed when you don't want to store the value in a format that is displayed on the screen, and you also don't want to display a screen in a format that is stored in the database. To overcome this problem, you need to perform a format conversion, but this is very difficult to do every time you display the field on a screen and update the field in a database. You can create conversion routines to perform input and output conversions automatically every time the value is entered or displayed on screen fields.

✓ And Here's How ...

Conversion routines are assigned to the domain definitions. You can open the domain definition in Transaction SE11 and assign a five-character identifier for the conversion routine as shown in Figure 1.

When you specify a conversion routine for a domain, two function modules are automatically assigned to the domain: one for input conversion and the other for output conversion. The function module names are automatically generated as follows, where *XXXXX* is the name of the conversion routine:

- ▶ `CONVERSION_EXIT_XXXXX_INPUT`
- ▶ `CONVERSION_EXIT_XXXXX_OUTPUT`

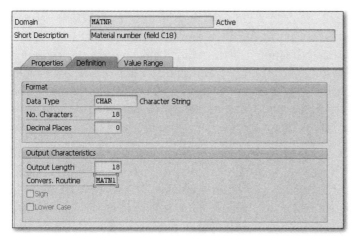

⩓ **Figure 1** *Conversion Routine Definition on a Domain Used for the Material Number Data Element*

For this example, assign the following two function modules to the domain:

▶ CONVERSION_EXIT_MATN1_INPUT

▶ CONVERSION_EXIT_MATN1_OUTPUT

The input function module converts from the display format to the internal format, and the output function module converts from the internal format to the display format. Both function modules have the same interface: INPUT as an input parameter and OUTPUT as an output parameter.

To create your own conversion routines, create two function modules according to the preceding definition. Then assign this conversion routine to your own domains. It's also possible to perform conversions using the function modules directly in the ABAP programs.

You can also use the conversion routines in the ABAP list programs with the WRITE command as follows:

WRITE belnr USING EDIT MASK '==ALPHA'.

You don't need to add a conversion routine to the write statement if it's already defined in the domain of the variable.

You can also override the conversion routine defined in the domain of the variable by using the following syntax:

WRITE belnr USING NO EDIT MASK.

In this example, we used the ALPHA conversion, which is defined in the system and used commonly to perform format conversion between external and internal numbers. It checks whether the input contains only digits ignoring the preceding and trailing spaces. If yes, it removes the preceding and trailing spaces, right aligns the number, and puts zeros in the remaining blanks on the left. For example, if you run the ALPHA conversion for a five-character string ' 123 ' it will be converted to '00123'. You can create your own conversion routine to perform the similar technique for custom fields according to your requirements.

Conversion routines are also automatically run on the screen fields if the conversion routine is assigned to the domain of the screen field. If you want to override the conversion routine or assign a conversion routine to a field that doesn't have a conversion routine assigned on a domain level, you can use the CONV. EXIT field on the dictionary attributes of the screen element as shown in Figure 2.

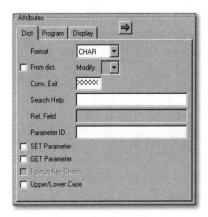

《 Figure 2 *Assigning a Conversion Routine to a Screen Element*

Make sure the FROM DICT. checkbox isn't selected; otherwise, the CONV. EXIT field is disabled because the system will use the default conversion exit that comes from the domain definition.

Creating a Secondary Index to Improve Table Access Performance

You can create secondary indexes to improve access to tables when you need to access a database table with the fields that don't exist in the primary key.

When you create a database table and assign a primary key, the primary index is automatically created in the database and is used for efficient access to the table. You can compare this to a book index that provides quick access to the area of your interest. You must provide the primary key fields in the queries that access the table to be able to use the primary index. However, sometimes you need to access a database table using a field that isn't a primary key. You can create a secondary index for this field(s) using ABAP Data Dictionary tools to improve your ability to access your tables.

✅ And Here's How ...

When you want to access a record in a table using the primary keys, the database manager first looks at the primary index. Because the index table is sorted by the primary keys, it easily queries the table and gets the position of the original record. The remaining job is just going to the main table and getting the requested row easily by using the position that you found on the index table. Figure 1 shows an example table with a primary index.

Suppose that you have a products table like that in Figure 1, and you want to access a record with product number MN22625. The database manager first looks at the primary index table. Because it's sorted by product, it easily finds row number 4 and uses it to find the main record on the main table.

Primary Key

#	Product	Category	Description
1	NB12345	Laptops	XY 15'' i7 Processor 8GB Memory
2	MN83112	Printers	PR all-in-one
3	NN82363	Networking	NN Dual-Band Wireless-N Router
4	MN22625	Monitors	MN 27'' Widescreen LCD Monitor
5	LH63938	Desktops	AS 13'' i5 Processor 4GB Memory

Primary Index

#	Product
5	LH63938
4	MN22625
2	MN83112
1	NB12345
3	NN82363

≫ *Figure 1 Example Selection with Primary Index*

However, when you try to access the same table using the CATEGORY field, which isn't a primary key, the database manager queries the main table directly to find the matching record. However, it can take a very long time to access data from large tables without using the primary key. Luckily, we can create secondary indexes to provide alternative access to the tables.

Access the secondary indexes of a table using the INDEXES button on the CHANGE TABLE screen in Transaction SE11. This will trigger a popup that displays the list of secondary indexes. Click the CREATE button (   ) to start creating a new index. Specify a three-character index ID, and click CONTINUE. The CREATE INDEX screen opens as shown in Figure 2, where you can specify the details for the index.

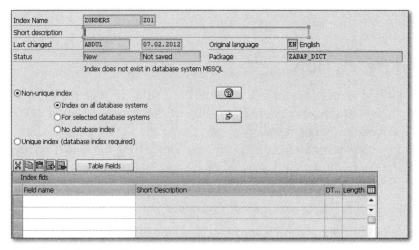

≫ *Figure 2 Creating a Secondary Index*

Fill in the SHORT DESCRIPTION field, and specify the index fields in the table. If the index fields uniquely identify a record in a table, select the UNIQUE INDEX radio button. Otherwise, select NON-UNIQUE INDEX, and choose one of the following three options:

▶ INDEX ON ALL DATABASE SYSTEMS
The index will be created physically on the database regardless of the database system.

▶ FOR SELECTED DATABASE SYSTEMS
You can select (or exclude) the list of the database systems in which the index will be created.

▶ NO DATABASE INDEX
The index will not be physically created on the underlying database. These types of indexes are optional indexes created only in the ABAP Data Dictionary, and they are helpful in certain conditions.

Save the index, and exit when you finish providing details.

Now, another table is created for the secondary index. The Database Manager decides which index will be used when you query the table. Let's extend the database table that you used in Figure 1 by creating a secondary index for the CATEGORY column. Suppose that you want to query the table with the CATEGORY field. Now, because the category isn't included in the primary index, the selection is performed through the secondary index as shown in Figure 3. The performance will be almost the same as using the primary index.

Primary Key

#	Product	Category	Description
1	NB12345	Laptops	XY 15" i7 Processor 8GB Memory
2	MN83112	Printers	PR all-in-one
3	NN82363	Networking	NN Dual-Band Wireless-N Router
4	MN22625	Monitors	MN 27" Widescreen LCD Monitor
5	LH63938	Desktops	AS 13" i5 Processor 4GB Memory

Secondary Index

#	Category
5	Desktops
1	Laptops
4	Monitors
3	Networking
2	Printers

Primary Index

#	Product
5	LH63938
4	MN22625
2	MN83112
1	NB12345
3	NN82363

☆ *Figure 3* Example Selection with Secondary Index

As you can see in Figure 3, every additional index consumes extra space in the database. You should only create a secondary index if it's necessary. Be sure to consider the size of the index that will be generated for large tables. It also affects the insert/update performance on the table because the indexes must be updated when the original table changes.

Extending Table Maintenance Dialogs with Events

You can use events in table maintenance dialogs to extend functionality by adding ABAP routines at specific events according to the customer's custom requirements.

The Table Maintenance Generator is a special tool in the ABAP Workbench designed to create table maintenance dialogs to maintain data in database tables or views. Although the generated dialogs are enough to maintain the table/view, but sometimes you may need to extend the functionalities of the maintenance dialogs according to the specific requirements. In this tip, we'll show you how to implement extended table maintenance events in predefined points to add additional logic to the maintenance dialogs.

✓ And Here's How ...

Table maintenance dialogs have many events that you can use to customize the functionality of the maintenance dialogs. Follow these steps:

1. Create the table maintenance dialog as described in Tip 61.
2. After creating the standard maintenance dialog, use extended table maintenance events to add your own logic. You can customize events using the following menu path:

ENVIRONMENT • MODIFICATION • EVENTS

A maintenance dialog opens, and you can create a new record for each event that you want to use. You'll notice that this is also the table maintenance dialog that is used to maintain the events that are called dynamically from the table maintenance dialog.

3. Let's create a simple example to see what you can do using events. Suppose that you have a table that is maintained by end users, and you want to store the username and current date every time the data is changed. Click the NEW ENTRIES button and select the event from the list as shown in Figure 1.

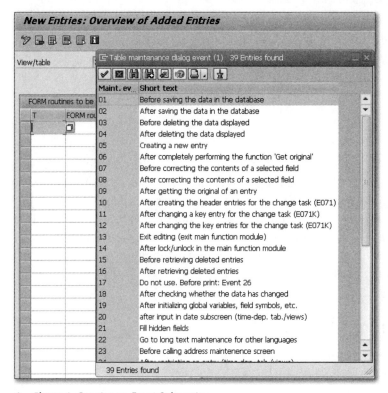

⌃ *Figure 1* *Creating an Event Subroutine*

As you can see in Figure 1, there are more than 30 events that you can use for different purposes. For this example, use event 01 to put additional information into the table just before it's saved in the database.

4. Select event 01, and specify the name of the subroutine that will run when the event is triggered in the FORM ROUTINE column. Click the empty button in the EDITOR column to open the editor where you can write the ABAP code.

5. As an example, write the following code to add current date and current time into the `erdat` and `ernam` fields before saving the record into Table zabap_dict1:

```
FORM before_save.
  DATA BEGIN OF wa_total.
          INCLUDE STRUCTURE zabap_dict1.
  DATA: action,
        mark,
  END OF wa_total.
  zabap_dict1-erdat = sy-datum.
  zabap_dict1-ernam = sy-uname.
  LOOP AT total INTO wa_total.
    IF <action> EQ 'U' OR
       <action> EQ 'N'.
      wa_total-erdat = sy-datum.
      wa_total-ernam = sy-uname.
      MODIFY total FROM wa_total.
      READ TABLE extract WITH KEY <vim_xtotal_key>.
      IF sy-subrc IS INITIAL.
        extract = wa_total.
        MODIFY extract INDEX sy-tabix.
      ENDIF.
    ENDIF.
  ENDLOOP.
ENDFORM.
```

You can modify the ABAP code to perform additional operations. For example, you can store the creation and modification dates into the different columns by distinguishing the processing state from predefined field symbol `<action>`.

6. Save and activate the source code. Now the `before_save` subroutine will be called from table maintenance dialog whenever you add, modify, or delete a record.

There are plenty of events that you can use in different situations. These events allow you to avoid writing custom maintenance dialogs for table maintenance requirements that can't be satisfied by classical table maintenance generation tools.

Tip 68

Creating View Clusters to Group Maintenance Dialogs Together for Better Maintenance

You can create view clusters to group several maintenance dialogs that belong to a single business function in one maintenance cluster.

Table maintenance dialogs allow you to maintain and transport business data in database tables. Although the maintenance dialogs are simple and easy to use, sometimes it can be difficult to maintain business data that resides in multiple tables. You can create view clusters for these tables to group maintenance dialogs in a single maintenance cluster for easier maintenance.

✔ And Here's How ...

View clusters are used to combine maintenance dialogs that belongs to the same business function in a single maintenance unit whether they have a physical relationship or not. Figure 1 shows an example view cluster with five maintenance dialogs grouped in a single maintenance unit.

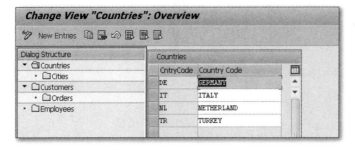

« *Figure 1* View Cluster Example

228

Let's say that you want to group tables in a single view cluster as in Figure 1 because of their similar business requirements. To create a view cluster, follow these steps:

1. Make sure each table you want to group has an individual maintenance dialog and can be maintained with Transaction SM30. If any are missing, create them in Transaction SE54 or Transaction SE11.

2. Go to Transaction SE54 and click the EDIT VIEW CLUSTER button on the toolbar.

3. Enter a new name for your view cluster and click the CREATE/CHANGE button. A screen opens as shown in Figure 2.

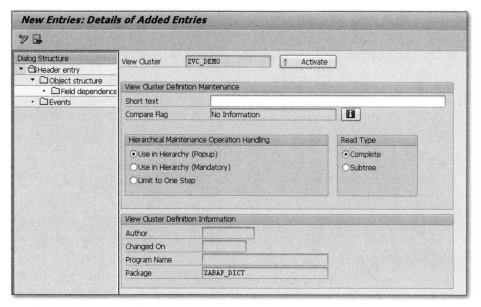

⌃ **Figure 2** *Create View Cluster*

4. Enter the description in the SHORT TEXT field, and then click the OBJECT STRUCTURE node on the left tree.

5. Enter the technical name of the maintenance dialogs into the VIEW/TABLE column of the OBJECT STRUCTURE list as shown in Figure 3, and fill other columns according to the following descriptions:

   ▸ SHORT TEXT: Enter the text that will describe the table in the hierarchy.

   ▸ PREDECESS.: Specify the higher element in the hierarchy. Enter the same object name if the current object is on the root level.

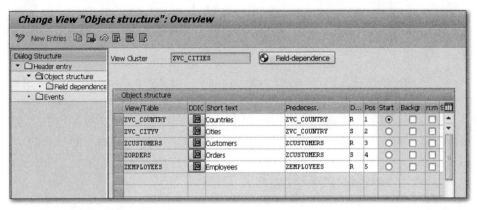

⤳ *Figure 3* *Build Object Structure*

▸ DEP: Specify how the dependent objects must be maintained according to the following definitions:

– R: The object is a header entry.

– S: You can select only one higher entry to maintain records in subtables.

– M: You can select multiple higher entries to maintain records in subtables.

▸ POS: Enter the line number in which the table will be displayed in the navigation hierarchy.

▸ START: Select the object that will be displayed on the top of the hierarchy.

6. Select all tables from the list, and click the GENERATE FIELD DEPENDENCE button (🌐 Field-dependence) to automatically generate field dependencies (this is a mandatory step). You can also select tables and click FIELD DEPENDENCE from the left navigation to maintain field dependencies manually. Figure 4 shows the field dependencies generated for our example.

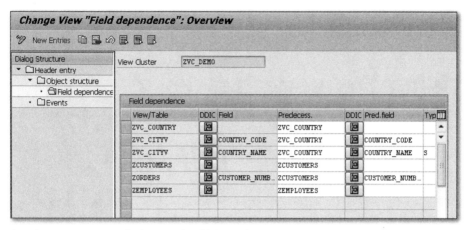

Change View "Field dependence": Overview

⤜ **Figure 4** *Automatically Generated Field Dependencies*

7. Go back to the header entry from the left navigation, and click ACTIVATE to generate the view cluster.

8. Go to Transaction SM34 to use the generated maintenance dialog.

Tip 69

Using Delivery Classes to Control the Transport Behavior of the Database Table Data

You can set different delivery class properties for database tables to categorize them, and thus control the delivery and transport behavior of table data.

SAP systems have huge numbers of database tables that contain customizing, transactional, and system data. Many additional database tables are also created by customers during the system implementation to store customer-specific data.

When a client copy, upgrade, language import, or a new installation needs to be performed, it's important to determine which database tables will be transported or overwritten. You can use the delivery class property to categorize the database tables and transport/overwrite behaviors that are determined according to this property. We'll also show you how to use this property to categorize custom database tables to specify the transport/overwrite behaviors.

✓ And Here's How ...

You can set the delivery class for a database table in the DELIVERY AND MAINTENANCE tab of the CHANGE TABLE screen in Transaction SE11. The following options can be selected for the delivery class:

► **A**
  Select this option for application tables that stores master and transactional data.

► **C**
  This option is used for customizing tables, which will be maintained only by customers.

- ▶ **L**

  Temporary tables that will store temporary data must be set to this option.

- ▶ **G**

  This option is used for customizing tables that must be protected against SAP updates. Only new data may be inserted during an SAP update.

- ▶ **E**

  This options is used for a control table. SAP and customers have separate key areas in these tables.

- ▶ **S**

  This option is used for system tables, which will be maintained only by SAP. Changes in these tables are treated as modification.

- ▶ **W**

  This option is used for system tables. The contents of these tables can be transported via separate objects.

These values affect the system behavior during installation, upgrade, client copy, and language import activities. Table 1 illustrates the system behavior for all possible conditions.

Delivery Class	Client Copy		Installation, Upgrade, and Language Import		
	Client Dependent	Client Independent	Client 000	Other Clients	Client Independent
A	Copy[1]	X	Insert & Overwrite	X	X
C	Copy	X	Insert & Overwrite	X	X
L	X	X	X	X	X
G	Copy	X	Insert & Overwrite	Insert	Insert
E	Copy	X	Insert & Overwrite	Insert & Overwrite	Insert & Overwrite
S	Copy	X	Insert & Overwrite	Insert & Overwrite	Insert & Overwrite
W	X	X	Insert & Overwrite	Insert & Overwrite	Insert & Overwrite

≫ *Table 1* *System Behaviors in Different Conditions*

---

1   Data is copied only if explicitly specified with the parameter option during the client copy.

You can see that if you create a client-dependent table with class L and W, the table's contents aren't copied during client copy. All other types are transferred to the new client. Tables with delivery class A aren't copied to the target client, but you can explicitly set a parameter to copy the data also during the client copy.

Also note that if you create a client-independent table, the contents won't be transferred with the client copy.

The delivery class also affects the behavior of the extended table maintenance in Transaction SM30 in the following conditions:

▶ You can transport table data entered in this transaction for tables with delivery classes W and L.

▶ If you try to enter data into a table with delivery class G, the data is checked in Table TRESC, and the input is rejected if the namespace is violated.

▶ Delivery class value must be C for tables that will be maintained on a development or test system and transported to the production system with a transport request.

It's important to set the correct delivery class values to the custom database tables according to these definitions. If you don't set this value carefully, you won't get any error at first, but it can generate serious problems in the future during client copy or system upgrades.

Tip 70

Displaying and Analyzing Table Relationships in a Graphic

You can generate a graphical representation to analyze the relationships between database tables.

When you start a new development project with database tables that relate to each other, you usually create foreign-key relationships to identify the relationships and maintain the data integrity. If you're creating tables with many foreign-key relationships or analyzing software that has database tables with many foreign-key relationships, a common problem is figuring out the table relations with the tools that you used to create the tables. In this tip, we'll show you how to bypass this issue by using a graphical representation tool in the ABAP Data Dictionary to visualize the foreign-key relationships of a table.

✓ And Here's How ...

When you display or modify a database table in Transaction SE11, you can see the foreign-key relationships in the CHECK TABLE column in the ENTRY HELP/CHECK tab as shown in Figure 1.

Notice the check table definitions for the SFLIGHT table on this screen. However, you can't see the foreign-key definitions that use this table as a check table on the same screen.

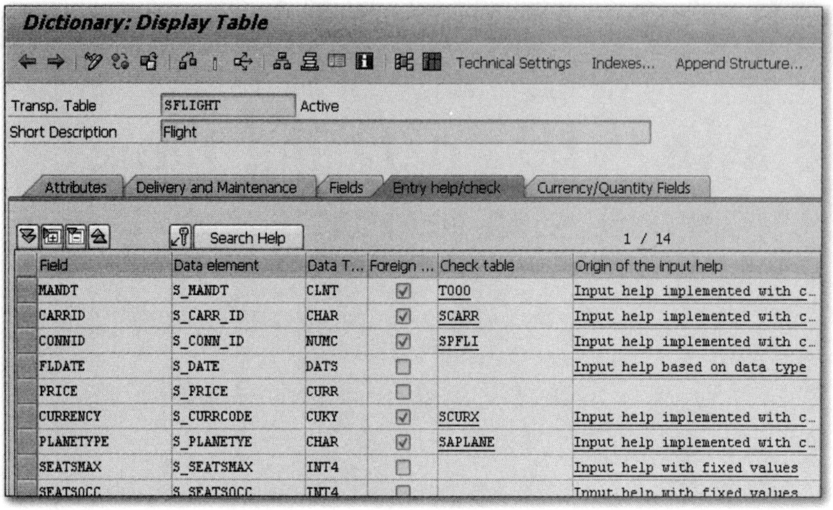

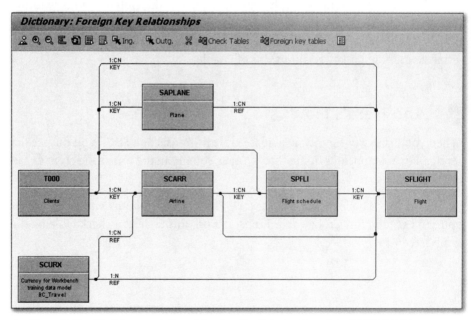

Figure 1 Foreign-Key Relationships of a Database Table

Now, say you want to draw the graphical representation of the foreign-key definitions of the SFLIGHT table. Click the GRAPHIC button (⊞) on the toolbar to see the graphic as shown in Figure 2.

Figure 2 Graphical Representation of Foreign-Key Relationships of the SFLIGHT Table

As you can see in Figure 2, tables that are defined as check tables in the fields of the SFLIGHT table are displayed. Table descriptions and cardinalities are also displayed in the graphic. You can use the following functions on the toolbar:

▶ If there are too many tables on the graphic, you can use the zoom functions on the toolbar to ZOOM IN (🔍) and ZOOM OUT (🔍).

▶ Use the HIDE function (✂) to hide the tables that you don't want to see on the graphic.

▶ Select any table from the graphic, and click the CHECK TABLES button to add the check tables of that table to the graphic.

▶ Select any table from the graphic, and click the FOREIGN KEY TABLES button to add the tables that use the selected table as a check table to the graphic.

▶ Select any table, and click the SELECT INGOING REL. button (🔲 Ing.) to highlight the tables that are used as a check table in the selected table.

▶ Select any table, and click the SELECT OUTGOING REL. button (🔲 Outg.) to highlight the tables that use the selected table as a check table.

▶ Click on any of the lines between the tables to open the foreign-key definition.

You can use this graphical representation to visually analyze the relationships between the database tables that are used in an application. For example, when you're trying to figure out the logic of an ABAP program that was developed by someone else, you can use this graphic to visualize the big picture and understand the business processes that lie behind the application. You can also add this graphic to the technical documentations to describe the database relations used in the software.

Tip (71)

Logging Data Changes in a Database Table

You can record and monitor the changes to the existing data records of a database table by enabling the logging indicator for that table.

Sometimes you need to log data changes to the database table that stores critical information. This is required particularly for auditing purposes, and it allows you to go back to any point in time and analyze the changes that have been made to the database records. Using the ABAP Data Dictionary, you can enable the logging for changes to the database table data and then analyze them in the future. This feature is used mostly to monitor the changes on the database tables that contain critical information.

✓ And Here's How ...

First, activate the table auditing feature from the system parameters to enable logging for database tables by using the `rec/client` parameter in the system parameters.

After making sure that the table auditing feature is active in the system, enable the function to log changes for a database table data. To do this, go to Transaction SE13, or use the TECHNICAL SETTINGS button on the DISPLAY/CHANGE TABLE screen in Transaction SE11; select the LOG DATA CHANGES checkbox in the table as shown in Figure 1.

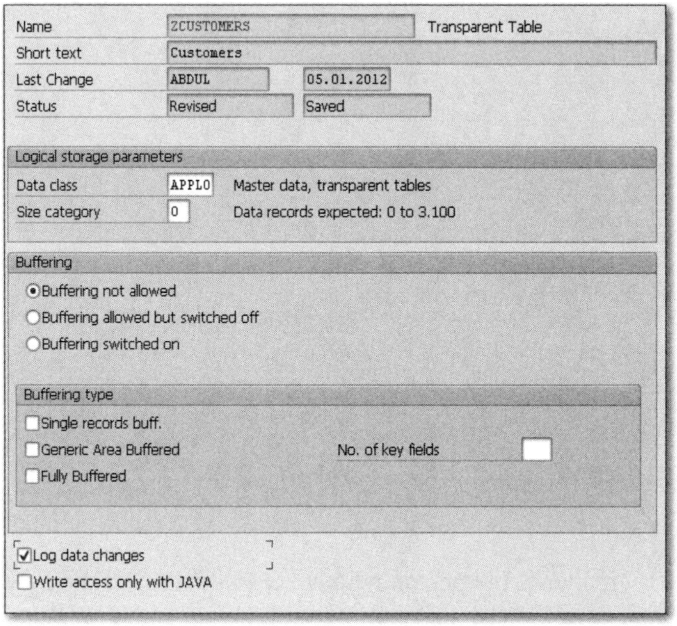

Figure 1 *Enabling the Logging for Data Changes*

Now, all changes to the records of the database table that are performed directly by a user or through an application are recorded in a log table; to display the logs, go to Transaction SCU3. You can also get the list of the logged tables using the LIST OF THE LOGGED TABLES button in Transaction SCU3.

Display the Log

To report the changes for a database table that has the LOG DATA CHANGES flag checked, follow these steps:

1. Go to Transaction SCU3.

2. Click the EVALUATE LOGS button in Transaction SCU3.

3. Enter the name of the table in the CUSTOMIZING OBJECT/TABLE field.

4. Adjust the start and end dates for the time range you're looking at, and run the report.

Figure 2 shows the sample Transaction SCU3 result that shows the changes in Table ZCUSTOMERS.

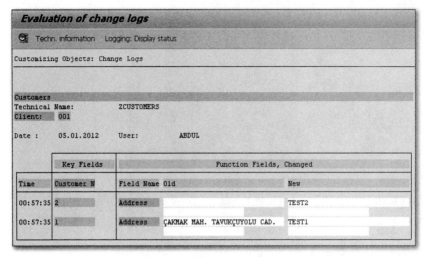

⏫ **Figure 2** *Evaluation of Change Logs*

Here, you can see the username of the person who changed the record, the time of the change, the key fields of the changed records, and the old and new values of the changed field.

Keep in mind the potential performance drawbacks of logging the changes. Whenever a change occurs on a table that is flagged to log changes, a new record is added to the log table. This can produce a very high load on the system if you log the changes for a table that is updated frequently by many users.

Linking Text Tables to Main Tables to Use Multi-Language Applications

To maintain and use applications that will be read in several languages, you can create text tables to store language-dependent information and then link those tables to the main tables.

When you're developing an application that will be used in different languages, a lot of information will change according to the user's language. This is much more than translating the screen texts into multiple languages—you must also consider the language-specific business information that must be maintained in different languages such as country names or currency names. We'll show you how to create text tables and bind the key information of the main table to the different values in the text tables depending on the user's logon language.

And Here's How ...

Suppose you're creating a table that will contain country codes and country names. Normally, you could create a table and add the country code and country name columns to that table. However, if the table will be used in more than one language, you have to maintain the country names for each language. The best way to do this, in terms of relational database design, is to create another table that will be linked to the main table with primary keys that contain additional language keys.

Follow these steps to create a country table and link a text table to the country table to store the country names:

1. Create the table to store the country keys in Transaction SE11 (note that the country names won't be stored in this table). To keep this example simple, only put the country code in the main table. Figure 1 shows the country table that contains the country key only.

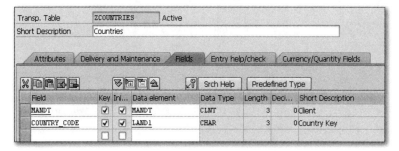

Transp. Table   ZCOUNTRIES   Active
Short Description   Countries

Attributes   Delivery and Maintenance   Fields   Entry help/check   Currency/Quantity Fields

Srch Help   Predefined Type

Field	Key	Ini...	Data element	Data Type	Length	Deci...	Short Description
MANDT	✓	✓	MANDT	CLNT	3	0	Client
COUNTRY_CODE	✓	✓	LAND1	CHAR	3	0	Country Key
	☐	☐					

≫ **Figure 1** *Country Table*

2. Create a second table with an additional language key (SPRAS). You can use the same table name but add "T" to the end (e.g., ZCOUNTRIEST) to describe that this is the text table of the ZCOUNTRIES table. Create the table as shown in Figure 2.

Transp. Table   ZCOUNTRIEST   Active
Short Description   Country Names

Attributes   Delivery and Maintenance   Fields   Entry help/check   Currency/Quantity Fields

Srch Help   Predefined Type

Field	Key	Ini...	Data element	Data Type	Length	Deci...	Short Description
MANDT	✓	✓	MANDT	CLNT	3	0	Client
SPRAS	✓	✓	SPRAS	LANG	1	0	Language Key
COUNTRY_CODE	✓	✓	LAND1	CHAR	3	0	Country Key
COUNTRY_NAME	☐	☐	ZCOUNTRY_NAME	CHAR	20	0	Country Name
	☐	☐					

≫ **Figure 2** *Text Table for the Country Table*

Notice that we only added the additional language column to the primary key and country name column to store the language-dependent country name.

3. Create a foreign-key relationship to link the current table as a text table of the country table. Select the COUNTRY_CODE row, and click the FOREIGN KEYS button (🔑). Fill in the details as shown in Figure 3.

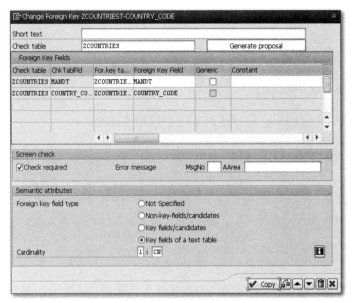

⌃ Figure 3 *Creating a Foreign Key to Link the Table to the Main Table as a Text Table*

Select the FOREIGN KEY FIELD TYPE as KEY FIELDS OF A TEXT TABLE, and select the proper cardinality. You can't select C cardinality on the left side because there must be a record in the check table that refers to the record in the text table. Otherwise, it would refer to an inconsistent record.

You've now created the text table to store country names and linked that table to the main country table.

4. Now you can use these two tables in the applications and create country names in as many languages as you like by creating records in the text table with different language keys.

Note that your end users won't even notice the existence of the text tables. For example, when you open the main table in Transaction SE16 (Data Browser), it's displayed as a single table and maintained in the user's logon language. You can only notice the language dependence by directly displaying the text table as shown in Figure 4.

Main Table		
MAN..	COUNTRY_CODE	COUNTRY_NAME
001	DE	GERMANY
001	TR	TURKEY
001	US	UNITED STATES

Text Table			
MAN..	SPRAS	COUNTRY_CODE	COUNTRY_NAME
001	E	DE	GERMANY
001	E	TR	TURKEY
001	E	US	UNITED STATES
001	T	DE	ALMANYA
001	T	US	AMERİKA
001	T	TR	TÜRKİYE

« Figure 4
Representation of Main Table and Text Table

243

Tip 73

Using Buffering Options for Database Tables to Improve System Performance

You can use buffering options for database tables to improve the access performance for tables that are used frequently.

If you're creating a database table that will be accessed frequently by system applications, you need to consider the quality of the access performance to the database table. Normally, whenever a record is requested from a database table, the application server must get this record from the database server. This operation can have a significantly negative effect on system performance. To avoid this issue, you can use some little-known buffering options for database tables to reduce database access by getting data from the buffer for frequently used tables. This will decrease unnecessary network load and increase overall system performance.

✓ And Here's How ...

Each database system has a buffering mechanism that's used to run SAP systems. However, application servers still need to access the database server to get the records whether it's in the database buffer or not. This increases the database server performance when responding to the request coming from the application server.

The SAP system has another buffer that resides in application servers; the servers use this buffer to obtain often-used data directly from the buffer without having to access the database server. This buffer leads to an additional increase in the system performance. If there's more than one application server, there are separate buffers on each. Figure 1 illustrates the buffering mechanism that's used in systems with more than one application server.

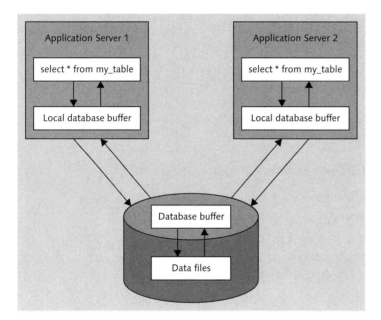

⌃ *Figure 1 Buffering Technique in SAP Systems*

If a change occurs in data buffered locally on the application servers, all other application servers are notified, and the buffers are updated asynchronously to avoid inconsistencies. If the buffered table is updated frequently on the system, this synchronization operation generates another load on the system. You must consider removing the buffer for these types of tables. Buffering is meaningful for tables that are read frequently but updated rarely.

Define Buffering Options

You can define buffering options in a database table that can be accessed through the Display Table screen in Transaction SE11 or Transaction SE13. Figure 2 shows the buffering options that can be selected.

> **Buffering**
> ◯ Buffering not allowed
> ◯ Buffering allowed but switched off
> ◉ Buffering switched on
>
> **Buffering type**
> ☐ Single records buff.
> ☐ Generic Area Buffered   No. of key fields ☐
> ☑ Fully Buffered

⌃ *Figure 2* *Buffering Options*

Choose from these buffering options:

▶ BUFFERING NOT ALLOWED
Buffering isn't allowed.

▶ BUFFERING ALLOWED BUT SWITCHED OFF
Buffering is technically possible, but the performance depends on certain conditions on the customer system. It's switched off initially but can be activated by the customer.

▶ BUFFERING SWITCHED ON
Buffering is switched on. The buffering type also must be specified for this case.

If you switch on buffering, you must also specify the buffering type. The following buffering types are available:

▶ SINGLE RECORDS BUFF.
The buffer is initially empty, but whenever a record is accessed, it's added to the record. This type of buffering is meaningful only when a few records of the table are accessed. It uses less space on the buffer than other buffer types.

▶ GENERIC AREA BUFFERED
When a record is accessed, all of the records that match with the first n key fields of the accessed data are buffered. You can define the number of key fields in the NO. OF KEY FIELDS field.

▶ FULLY BUFFERED
The buffer is initially empty, but all of the records are transferred to the buffer when a single access occurs to that table. Be careful about the table size when using this type of buffering.

Buffering is very useful to improve the system performance, but it can also be dangerous if you don't use it correctly. Consider using single record or generic area buffering for large tables.

The following statements bypass the buffer and go directly to the database:

▶ `Select` statement with a join or subquery

▶ Aggregate functions (`count`, `min`, `max`, `sum`, `avg`)

▶ `Group by`

▶ `Having`

▶ `Select Distinct`

▶ `Order By`

Sometimes, you may need to bypass the buffer for certain conditions. You can add the `bypassing buffer` option into the select statement to bypass the buffer and go directly to the database in such cases.

Using Lock Objects to Control Multi-User Access to Table Records

You can keep multiple users from accessing the same data records at the same time, and therefore avoid inconsistencies in the data, by setting lock objects within ABAP code.

When you're developing an application that requires inserts and updates to database tables, you need to stop users from accessing and changing the data in these tables while you're working. Otherwise, an inconsistency may occur if one user changes the data while the other user is using the unchanged version of the data. In this tip, we'll show you how to use lock objects to control this type of simultaneous access to the business data.

✓ And Here's How ...

A lock mechanism must be used in all applications that perform an update in business data. You can create a lock object by selecting the LOCK OBJECT option and clicking CREATE in Transaction SE11. Note that the naming convention is a little bit different for lock objects than the normal ABAP Workbench objects—the name must start with EZ or EY.

Suppose that you're developing an application that creates and updates the sales order data in database Table ZORDERS. A single order is identified with an order number, so you must lock the records that belong to that order number whenever a user enters the change screen for that order. If another user tries to modify the same order, an error message must be displayed to notify the user that the order is currently being edited by another user. This mechanism is used for all objects in SAP systems, and you can add the same functionality to your custom developments.

Let's create a lock object for Table ZORDERS:

1. Go to Transaction SE11.
2. Select LOCK OBJECT; enter the name of the lock object as "EZORDERS", and then click CREATE.
3. Enter the short description.
4. Select the checkbox ALLOW RFC if you want the generated functions to be called from outside.
5. Navigate to the TABLES tab, and enter the name of the table in the NAME field.
6. Select the appropriate lock mode. This will be used as a default value in the generated function module. You'll be able to specify other lock modes with the function module. The following options are available:

   ▸ **S: (shared lock)**
   More than one user can request and get this type of lock.

   ▸ **E: (exclusive lock)**
   Only one user can get this type of lock for an object at a time. If a user gets this type of lock for an object, all other requests for exclusive and shared locks are rejected. Further locks can only be requested by the lock owner.

   ▸ **X: (extended exclusive lock)**
   An extended version of the exclusive lock. The only difference is that all further locks are rejected even if the request is coming from the lock owner.

   ▸ **O: (optimistic lock)**
   This is the same as a shared lock but can be converted to an exclusive lock later in the transaction. This lock type is used when a transaction is opened in change mode but isn't likely to have an update in the transaction. If an update is triggered in the transaction, this lock is first converted to an exclusive lock by requesting a new lock with lock mode R for the same object, and the update is performed only if the lock is successfully converted to the exclusive lock.

   ▸ **R**
   This type of lock is requested to change the optimistic lock to the exclusive lock if an update must be triggered for an object.

▶ **C, U, V, W**

These lock modes are used only to perform collision checks. They don't set the lock but only return the result as if the lock is requested. It's like a test run. You can use the following lock modes to perform collision checks:

- Lock mode U is used to test lock mode X.
- Lock mode V is used to test lock mode E.
- Lock mode W is used to test lock mode S.
- Lock mode C is used to test lock mode R.

It's also possible to add other tables that will be locked together with the primary table to the Secondary Tables list. All of the secondary tables must be linked with foreign keys. Foreign-key relationships of the tables must be in a tree structure. Each subnode in a tree must be a check table of the higher node.

7. Navigate to the Lock parameter tab, and set the keys that will be used as import parameters in the function module that will be used to add or remove the table from the lock table. The system offers the keys of the lock table by default. You can make changes if you want.

8. Save (⊞) and activate (✶) the lock object.

The lock object is now ready to use. Two function modules are automatically generated:

▶ `ENQUEUE_EZORDERS` will be used to lock the table.

▶ `DEQUEUE_EZORDERS` will be used to release the locks on the table.

Now you can use these two functions in the ABAP programs to set and release locks for the business data.

Creating Alternative Search Help Paths with Collective Search Helps

You can offer alternative search paths to the user by combining several search helps into a single search help.

Search help is one of the most useful features of the ABAP Workbench, providing easy access to possible entries for screen fields. In a search help, a table or view must be defined to populate the possible values list, and the user can use the selection parameters to filter the list. Sometimes, there can be many different paths to populate the possible values list.

To allow users to use all search helps together, you can create a separate search help for all possible selection paths and combine these search helps into a *collective search help*. Collective search helps can be used to enhance the functionality of elementary search helps, and you can even implement your custom requirements with search help exits and generate search screens that would normally need too many lines of ABAP codes to be written.

✅ And Here's How ...

Elementary search helps must be created before creating the collective search helps. Each search help may have a different interface and selection tables, but all of these interfaces must be mapped to the main collective search help. However, it isn't necessary to use all interface parameters in each search help.

Figure 1 shows an example of a collective search help that's used to search for a sales order.

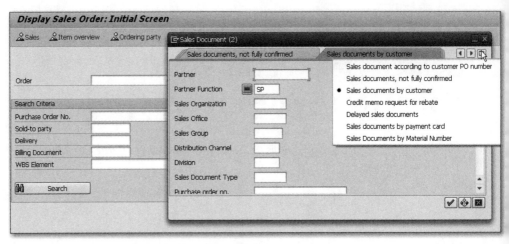

Figure 1 *Collective Search Help for a Sales Order*

As you can see in Figure 1, several search helps are defined in a single collective search help, and the user can use any of them by selecting from the list.

Let's create our custom collective search help for order selection by using the search helps provided for orders:

1. Go to Transaction SE11.

2. Select the SEARCH HELP radio button and enter "ZSH_ORDERS" in the text field.

3. Click CREATE.

4. Select COLLECTIVE SEARCH HELP on the popup and click CONTINUE.

5. Enter the short description for the search help, and enter "VBELN" as the search help parameter as shown in Figure 2.

6. Navigate to the INCLUDED SEARCH HELPS tab, and enter the name of all search helps in the SEARCH HELP list. For example, you can include the following search helps:

   ▶ VMVAB: Sales documents by description
   ▶ VMVAE: Sales documents by customer
   ▶ VMVMO: Sales documents by material number

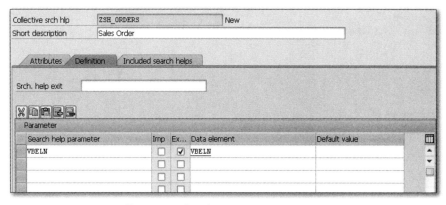

⏶ *Figure 2 Creating Collective Search Help*

7. Now you need to assign the interface parameters of each search help to the collective search help's interface parameters. Select the search help from the list, and click the PARAM. ASSIGNMENT button to assign the sales order document number from the included search help to the interface parameter.

8. A popup displays; click YES to confirm the proposal of the automatic parameter assignment.

9. Modify the proposed parameter assignment if needed, and click COPY to confirm the parameter assignment.

10. Save (🖫) and activate (🛉) the collective search help after you finish all parameter assignments.

11. Finally, click TEST (🖳) to see the generated search help.

You can now assign this collective search help to the fields for which end users might want alternative search options in certain cases.

Using Domains to Define Value Ranges for Database Tables and Structure Components

You can easily create reusable domains to define value ranges and technical settings for database fields and structure components.

When you create a database table or structure, you have three alternative ways to define technical characteristics for a database field or structure component. You can use the direct definition option or use data elements, but in both cases you have limited flexibility in the definition. To bypass this issue, you can create domains to define the technical settings and value ranges, and then reuse this domain for several database fields and structure components.

✓ And Here's How ...

You can create the domain by selecting the DOMAIN option in Transaction SE11. You can also create the domain using forward navigation within the DATA ELEMENT screen. Figure 1 shows the initial screen when you start creating a domain.

In the DEFINITION tab, define the format and output characteristics for a domain. Specify the data type and additional properties in the FORMAT section, and enter the output options in the OUTPUT CHARACTERISTICS section.

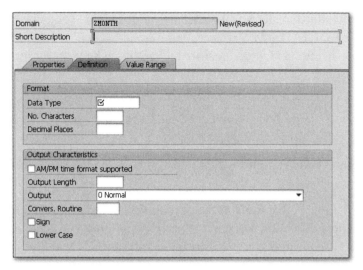

⋩ *Figure 1* Creating a Domain

Navigate to the VALUE RANGE tab. There are three types of value ranges that can be defined for a domain as shown in Figure 2.

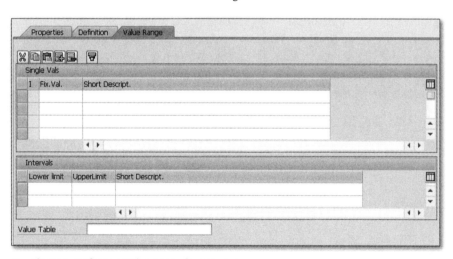

⋩ *Figure 2* Defining a Value Range for a Domain

If the possible values that the domain can take are fixed, and you can list by single entries, define the values in the SINGLE VALS part. For example, if you're defining a domain to use for the month field, you can enter the months as single values to this list.

Sometimes it may not be possible to define single values; instead, intervals can be defined in the INTERVALS part. For example, you can use a 0-100 interval for a domain that will be used for the percentage field.

You can add more than one interval into the list and also combine intervals with the single values.

You can also define a value table that contains the values that the field can take, but defining a value table here doesn't implement the value check. The value table is proposed as the check table when you create a foreign key for the field that linked to this domain.

Now you can reuse this domain in several data elements and use these data elements in database fields and structure components where you want to assign the value ranges defined in the domain.

Using value ranges in domains is very practical when the possible values that field can take won't change in time. If you enter fixed values into a domain, an automatic search help appears in all screen fields that use that domain. If a search help or foreign key are assigned to the field at a higher level, the value range defined in the domain is overridden by the higher level assignment.

Tip 77

Attaching Search Helps Directly to Data Elements for Global Availability

You can attach search helps to data elements to make the search help available globally for all fields that use that data element.

Search helps can be assigned to the screen elements in several ways. However, if you use the same data element in multiple screen elements, database fields, or structure components (which is common in SAP), it will be difficult to assign (or modify) the search help to all of these fields one by one.

In this tip, we'll show you how to attach a specific search help directly to the data elements. It will then be available for all screen elements, database fields, and structure components that use that data element, which will make the search help easier to assign and modify en masse.

And Here's How ...

Define a new data element or modify an existing one in Transaction SE11. Select the DATA TYPE radio button and navigate to the FURTHER CHARACTERISTICS tab. Here you can define the search help name and parameter as shown in Figure 1.

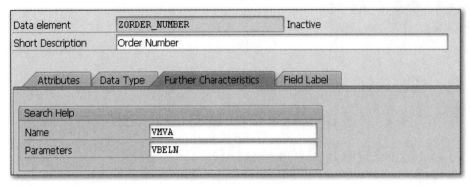

⌃ *Figure 1* *Assigning a Search Help to the Data Element*

Enter the name of the search help in the NAME field, and enter the export parameter of the search help in the PARAMETERS field.

If the assigned parameter is also an import parameter, the value of the field is transferred to the search help as an import parameter when you trigger the search help. However, if there is more than one import parameter in the search help, only the selected import parameters are used in the search help. All of the other parameters are treated as empty.

This type of search help definition allows you to define a search help in a data element and assign it to multiple objects that are linked to this data element. You can also make this assignment one by one to the relevant objects if you're working on a small application. However, if the same data element will be used by many developers, and you don't want them to lose time by dealing with the same tasks, you can assign the search help to the data element.

Note that you can override the search help definition on the data element by assigning another search help on the database field, structure component, or screen element.

Tip 78

Adding Date Fields to Make Time-Sensitive Table Maintenance Dialogs

You can maintain records that are valid for limited time periods by using special functions within table maintenance dialogs.

Sometimes you may need to create a database table to store business information that is only valid for a specific time span. You must also ensure that these tables contain one valid record at a time at the most. When it comes to maintaining the records of these tables, the standard table maintenance dialogs are difficult to use because limiting the validity of one record manually and creating another record with a new validity period can be frustrating and error-prone. Luckily, there are special functions in table maintenance dialogs to handle the validity of the time-dependent records, which we discuss in this tip.

✓ And Here's How ...

In a time-dependent database table, you must be able to create more than one record with different validity periods for the same business data and ensure that only one of those records is valid at a time. You can handle this situation by adding two date fields to identify the validity period of the record and adding one of these fields to the primary key to be able to create more than one record for the same data.

When creating a time-dependent database table, the following conditions must be satisfied:

- ▶ The table must contain two fields to represent start and end dated for the validity period of a record.

- ▶ One of these fields must be in the key field, and the other field must be the first field after the primary key. This allows you to insert more than one record for the same business data.

- ▶ The START DATE field must have one of the following data elements:
  - ▶ BEGDA
  - ▶ BEGDATUM
  - ▶ VIM_BEGDA

- ▶ The END DATE field must have one of the following data elements:
  - ▶ ENDDA
  - ▶ ENDDATUM
  - ▶ VIM_ENDDA

After you create a table and generate the table maintenance dialogs, choose ENVIRONMENT • GENERATE TIME-DEP. to generate time dependence while you're in the Table Maintenance Generator. If you forget to run this step, some of the time-dependence functions will still be available, but they won't run as expected.

Now, enter the table maintenance dialog in Transaction SM30. You'll notice two new buttons added on the toolbar as shown in Figure 1.

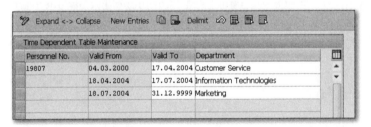

≫ **Figure 1** *Table Maintenance Dialog for Time-Dependent Table*

Normally, you have to create custom table maintenance programs to handle time-dependence, but this technique allows you to create table maintenance dialogs to maintain time-dependent data easily while preserving the data integrity.

The following tools will help you further manage the time sensitivity of your business information:

▶ EXPAND <-> COLLAPSE button
  Allows you to collapse the records to show only the valid record for the current
  date. If there isn't a valid record, the last record will be shown. You can later
  select the record and use the same button to expand the records.

▶ DELIMIT button
  Allows you to create a new record starting from a specific date and delimit the
  current valid record to the start date of the new record.

When you try to create a record that overlaps with another record, the system automatically restricts the validity of the existing record to preserve the data integrity.

Tip 79

Using the Database Utility to Transfer Structural Changes to the Database System

You can prevent data loss by using the database utility to apply the structural changes in database tables to the underlying database system.

The ABAP Data Dictionary allows SAP systems to interact with the database tables independently of the underlying relational database system. Tables, views, and other dictionary objects have runtime objects that are used by ABAP programs to access the database tables. These runtime objects store the technical information about database objects and provide considerable increases in system performance during database access.

If you make a structural change to the database tables in the ABAP Data Dictionary, the changes can't be applied directly to the database system and an adjustment may be required to prevent the possible data losses. In this tip, we'll show you how to use the database utility to perform this adjustment.

✓ And Here's How ...

When you create a database table, view, or other dictionary element in the ABAP Data Dictionary, a runtime object is generated in the ABAP workbench to store information about the created object. ABAP programs use these runtime objects to access information from these objects. The runtime objects are regenerated whenever a dictionary object is activated in the ABAP Data Dictionary.

You can display the corresponding runtime object of dictionary objects by opening the maintenance screen for the object in Transaction SE11 and using the following menu path:

UTILITIES • RUNTIME OBJECT • DISPLAY

Figure 1 shows a runtime object for a database table.

Transparent table	Timestamp runtime object
ZAG_RO_DEMO	08.01.2012 22:04:01
Timestamp ABAP	Timestamp DYNP
08.01.2012 22:03:54	08.01.2012 22:03:54

Header of active runtime object

Obj	Dat	No.	Tabl	No.	Key	Pos	Alig	Buff	Nu	Len	Flag 1	P	DB	Flag 2	Flag 3	Flag 4	Flag 5	Flag 6	Pol	Uni	UUID	Leaf
T	T	3	126	2	26	1	2		0	0	00000010		B	00000010	00000000	00000000	00000100	00000000	0	2	E13A33E381A705F1	0

Fields of active runtime object

Field Name	Fiel	Dep	Data	ABA	DB leng	Dec	Field	Out	Fiel	AB	ABA	Dict	Flag 1	Flag 2	Flag 3	Flag 4	Data ele	Pre	R	R	Conv	Para	C
MANDT	1	0	CLNT	6	6	0	0	3	152	0	C	0	01000001	00000000	00000000	00000000	MANDT	0					
KUNNR	2	0	CHAR	20	20	0	6	10	40	0	C	0	01100001	00000110	00000010	00000000	KUNNR	0			ALPHA	KUN	
NAME1	3	0	CHAR	100	100	0	26	50	40	0	C	0	00000100	00000000	00000000	00000000	TEXT50	0					

≋ **Figure 1** Runtime Object for a Database Table

If you change the structure of a table in the ABAP Data Dictionary, the database object is adjusted in the following ways depending on the type of the change, database system used, and whether the table is empty or not:

▸ If only the order of the non-key columns is changed, the runtime object is updated, but there is no need to update the column orders in the database.

▸ If the table is empty, it's deleted and recreated in the database.

▸ If the table isn't empty, the system performs the change using the ALTER TABLE command.

▸ If the result of the ALTER TABLE command isn't successful, the table conversion must be run in the database utility.

Conversion Process
If you make a structural change in the database table that requires a data-conversion process according to the preceding conditions, an error message is displayed as shown in Figure 2 when you try to activate the table in the ABAP Data Dictionary.

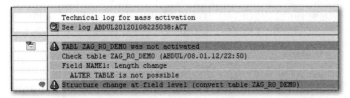

```
        Technical log for mass activation
      See log ABDUL20120108225038:ACT

      TABL ZAG_RO_DEMO was not activated
        Check table ZAG_RO_DEMO (ABDUL/08.01.12/22:50)
        Field NAME1: Length change
          ALTER TABLE is not possible
      Structure change at field level (convert table ZAG_RO_DEMO)
```

⌃ *Figure 2 Activation Error Received When the Structure of the Table is Changed*

The conversion process can be performed using the following procedure in the database utility:

1. Go to Transaction SE14, and enter the name of the table in the Obj. Name field.
2. Select the Tables option in the Dictionary Objects selection, and click the Edit button.
3. In the next screen, select one of the following processing types to run the conversion process:
   - ▶ Direct: Conversion runs directly.
   - ▶ Background: Conversion runs in the background.
   - ▶ Enter for mass processing: Puts the object into the mass processing list, which can be processed later.
4. Select whether the data should be saved or deleted during conversion, and click Activate and adjust database to start (or schedule) the conversion process.

After you start the conversion, if you selected to delete the data option, the table is deleted and recreated with the new structure. If you selected to save the data, the conversion process runs by performing the following steps:

1. The original table is renamed to a temporary table, and all indexes are deleted.
2. The new table is created with the new definition.
3. Old data is copied from the temporary table using the move-corresponding logic as in ABAP.
4. The temporary table is deleted.
5. The secondary indexes are recreated.

During the conversion process, the table is locked to prevent data inconsistencies in the programs that use this table.

Tip 80

Defining Ranges Using Range Table Types

You can build better database queries by using range table types to create range types and use them in the interface parts of the classes and function modules.

Ranges types are very useful in ABAP programs because they allow you to create special internal tables that can be used to build complex selection criteria easily and use it in logical conditions in statements such as select, loop, and so on. Range type variables are generated automatically with the select-options statement in report programs, or you can explicitly define them using the range command. In this tip, we'll show you how you can create range table types in the ABAP Data Dictionary in order to transfer range types among programs, function modules, and classes.

✓ And Here's How ...

A range table type is a special type of table type that is defined in almost the same way as normal table types. You can create range table types by performing the following steps:

1. Go to Transaction SE11 and select the DATA TYPE option. Enter the name of the RANGE TABLE TYPE and click CREATE.
2. Select the TABLE TYPE option and click CONTINUE.
3. Enter a short description.
4. Change the table type to the range table type by choosing EDIT • DEFINE AS RANGES TABLE. The screen changes as shown in Figure 1.

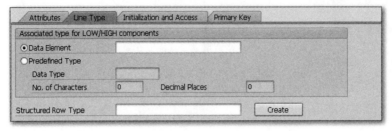

⌃ *Figure 1* *Defining the Range Table Type*

5. Fill in the details for the type—you must set the data type that will be used to build the range type. You can either specify DATA ELEMENT or use PREDEFINED DATA TYPE. This type defines the elementary type of the LOW and HIGH fields of the range table.

6. Assign a row type just like you would in normal table types. You can generate it automatically by entering the name in the STRUCTURED ROW TYPE and clicking the CREATE button. This creates a structure using the specified DATA ELEMENT you defined in the previous step. In our example, we used KUNNR as the data element. The structure is created as shown in Figure 2.

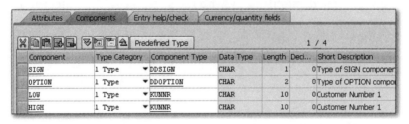

⌃ *Figure 2* *Creating a Structure for the Line Type of Range Table Type*

You can also use the previously created structure and assign it to the range table type in the definition screen.

7. Save (🖫) and activate (🔃) the object.

Now, you can use it in the function module or class interfaces and handle the complex logical conditions in statements such as Select, Loop, If, and so on.

Using the Data Modeler to Create Data Models According to the SAP SERM Method

You can display complex data models in a clear and easily understandable way by using the Data Modeler tool to create data models.

When you're designing an object-oriented (OO) application, data modeling is a good start to define the business requirements, identify business objects, and create a data model that will be used as a reference throughout the implementation phase. The ABAP Workbench has a Data Modeler tool that you can use to create data models according to the SAP SERM (Structured Entity Relationship Model) method.

The Data Modeler is a very useful tool not only to create data models for designing an application, but also to document the data model for your existing application. A lot of developers find it difficult and tedious to create documentation for their applications; however, they can use data models to create documentations and keep them up to date because the models are closely integrated with the ABAP Data Dictionary. In this tip, we'll show you how to use the Data Modeler tool to create data models according to the SAP SERM method.

✔️ And Here's How ...

You can use both top-down and bottom-up approaches for data modeling while using the Data Modeler.

Different Approaches

In the top-down approach, the modeling starts with creating entities and specifying attributes for these entities. Then, you can link entities to the tables and views in the ABAP Data Dictionary. You can either use the existing tables or views or create new tables or views for the entity types. The attributes of the entities are linked to the fields of the tables and views. If you add a new field to the table or view, it can also be seen in the Data Modeler.

In the bottom-up approach, you start with the existing application and create a data model for the existing tables and views in the application.

Working with the Data Modeler

You can access the Data Modeler tool from Transaction SD11 or by using the following path in the SAP menu:

TOOLS • ABAP WORKBENCH • DEVELOPMENT • DATA MODELER

On the initial screen, there are links to the SAP applications and SAP architecture that allow you to see the existing data model and views of the SAP system.

You can create entities and include these entities in the data models with suitable relations.

In Figure 1, you can see the existing data model BC_TRAVEL, which is created for the flight model.

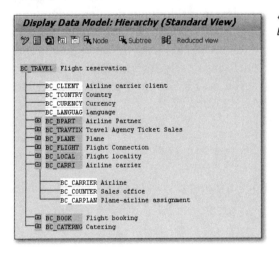

《 Figure 1 *Hierarchical Display for the BC_TRAVEL Data Model*

The model contains entities and submodels. For example, BC_CARRI is a submodel that describes the AIRLINE CARRIER data model, which contains three entities. Double-click on the BC_CARRI submodel to see the definition of the submodel. In the definition screen, clicking on the GRAPHIC button (🔲) shows you the graphical display of the AIRLINE CARRIER data model as shown in Figure 2.

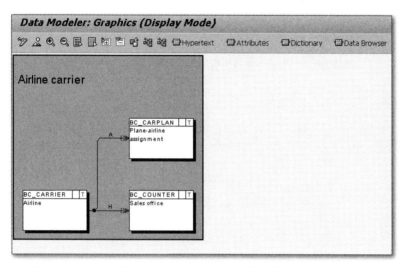

Figure 2 *Graphical Display of the Data Model BC_CARRI*

There are three entities in the model, and you can also see the relationships and relationship types on the graphic. The relationships are defined according to the following definitions:

- **A**: Aggregating
- **H**: Hierarchical
- **R**: Referential
- **X**: External

The link between the entities specifies that the target entity depends on the source entity according to the relationship types described previously. The arrow on the relationship link also defines the cardinality of the dependent entity type according to the following definitions:

- **Single arrow: Cardinality 1**
  Each source entity has exactly one dependent entity.

► **Vertical line + single arrow: Cardinality C**
Each source entity has a maximum of one dependent entry.

► **Double arrow: Cardinality N**
Each source entity has at least one dependent entry.

► **Vertical line + double arrow: Cardinality CN**
Each source entity has any number of dependent entities.

You can also access the attributes, dictionary assignments, and Data Browser for the entity by selecting it and using the appropriate button on the toolbar.

Part 8

Enhancements

Things You'll Learn in this Section

In the SAP system, you can adjust standard programs according to customer or business requirements in several ways. One of the greatest features that SAP provides developers to enhance standard programs is the Enhancement Framework. You can use the tools provided in the Enhancement Framework to change the system standard without modifying the standard programs. This part of the book provides tips and tricks about using different ABAP Workbench techniques that enhance out-of-the-box functionality.

Enhancing Standard Objects with Implicit Enhancement Options

You can pinpoint code points that are suitable for enhancement by enhancing standard ABAP programs at specific places in the source code.

There are many enhancement points and enhancement sections placed in predefined locations in the standard ABAP programs that can be used to enhance the system. However, it isn't always possible to find a suitable enhancement point in the source code that needs to be enhanced. The Enhancement Framework allows you to change standard system functionality by modifying the ABAP source code according to your client's custom requirements. We'll show you how to use implicit enhancement options in these cases, which allow you to enhance the source code at specific points in the ABAP programs without modifying existing ABAP code.

And Here's How ...

You can use implicit enhancement options if there are no suitable explicit enhancement options available in the source code. Implicit enhancement options are located in the source code so that you'll likely never need to modify the original objects again. You can find implicit enhancement options in the following places:

At the End of ...	At the Beginning and End of ...
▶ Includes ▶ Public, private, and protected sections of a local classes ▶ Implementation section of local classes ▶ Interface definitions ▶ Structure definitions ▶ Changing, importing, and exporting parameter list of a method in local classes	▶ Form routines ▶ Function modules ▶ Methods ▶ Enhancement implementations (nested enhancements)

Let's implement an example implicit enhancement. Suppose that you want to enhance demo Program BCALV_FULLSCREEN_DEMO to add an additional comment line to the list header shown in Figure 1.

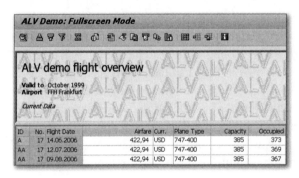

«   Figure 1 *ALV List Header to be Enhanced*

When you analyze the source code, you can easily see that the header is built in the subroutine COMMENT_BUILD:

```
FORM COMMENT_BUILD USING LT_TOP_OF_PAGE TYPE
                                    SLIS_T_LISTHEADER.
  DATA: LS_LINE TYPE SLIS_LISTHEADER.
  ...
  LS_LINE-TYP  = 'A'.
* LS_LINE-KEY:  NOT USED FOR THIS TYPE
  LS_LINE-INFO = TEXT-105.
  APPEND LS_LINE TO LT_TOP_OF_PAGE.
ENDFORM.
```

Thus, if you can add your comments to internal Table LT_TOP_OF_PAGE, your comments will be visible in the report header.

As we mentioned, there must be implicit enhancement options at the beginning and the end of the subroutine. You can see this using the following menu path:

EDIT • ENHANCEMENT OPERATIONS • SHOW IMPLICIT ENHANCEMENT OPTIONS

The implicit enhancement options are displayed as lines with quotes as shown in Figure 2.

```
130  ⊟ FORM COMMENT_BUILD USING LT_TOP_OF_PAGE TYPE
131                        SLIS_T_LISTHEADER.
132    """"""""""""""""""""""""""""""""""""""""""""""""""""""""""""""""""""""""""""""""""""""""""$"$\SE:(10) Form COMMENT
133      DATA: LS_LINE TYPE SLIS_LISTHEADER.
134  ⊟ *
135    * LIST HEADING LINE: TYPE H
136      CLEAR LS_LINE.
137      LS_LINE-TYP  = 'H'.
138    * LS_LINE-KEY:  NOT USED FOR THIS TYPE
139      LS_LINE-INFO = TEXT-100.
140      APPEND LS_LINE TO LT_TOP_OF_PAGE.
141    * STATUS LINE: TYPE S
142      CLEAR LS_LINE.
143      LS_LINE-TYP  = 'S'.
144      LS_LINE-KEY  = TEXT-101.
145      LS_LINE-INFO = TEXT-102.
146      APPEND LS_LINE TO LT_TOP_OF_PAGE.
147      LS_LINE-KEY  = TEXT-103.
148      LS_LINE-INFO = TEXT-104.
149      APPEND LS_LINE TO LT_TOP_OF_PAGE.
150    * ACTION LINE: TYPE A
151      CLEAR LS_LINE.
152      LS_LINE-TYP  = 'A'.
153    * LS_LINE-KEY:  NOT USED FOR THIS TYPE
154      LS_LINE-INFO = TEXT-105.
155      APPEND LS_LINE TO LT_TOP_OF_PAGE.
156    """"""""""""""""""""""""""""""""""""""""""""""""""""""""""""""""""""""""""""""""""""""""""$"$\SE:(11) Form COMMENT
157  └ ENDFORM.
```

⌃ **Figure 2** *Displaying Implicit Enhancement Options for Subroutines*

You can now add your ABAP code just before the ENDFORM statement to be able to add your comments to internal Table LT_TOP_OF_PAGE.

Click the ENHANCE button (⊚) on the toolbar to turn the ABAP Editor into enhancmement mode. Now, implicit enhancement options can also be identified with the ⬛➡ sign on the left of the line. Position the cursor on the enhancement option just before ENDFORM, and use the following menu path to start the enhancement operation:

EDIT • ENHANCEMENT OPERATIONS • CREATE IMPLEMENTATION

Now, follow these steps:

1. Select CODE as the type of enhancement in the CHOOSE ENHANCEMENT MODE popup.

2. Enter a name in the ENHANCEMENT IMPLEMENTATION field, enter the description in the SHORT TEXT field, and then click the CONTINUE button (✓) to continue.

3. Enter a package and save.

4. Enter the transport request.

5. Write your code between the ENHANCEMENT / ENDENHANCEMENT statements as shown in Figure 3.

```
151  * ACTION LINE: TYPE A
152      CLEAR LS_LINE.
153      LS_LINE-TYP   = 'A'.
154  * LS_LINE-KEY:   NOT USED FOR THIS TYPE
155      LS_LINE-INFO = TEXT-105.
156      APPEND LS_LINE TO LT_TOP_OF_PAGE.
157  """""""""""""""""""""""""""""""""""""""""""""""""""""""""""""""""""""
158  *$*$-Start: 9999-----------------------------------------------------
159  ENHANCEMENT 1  ZIMPLICIT_ENHANCEMENT.      "inactive version
160      CLEAR LS_LINE.
161      LS_LINE-TYP = 'A'.
162      LS_LINE-INFO = '100 Things You Should Know About ABAP Workbench'.
163      APPEND LS_LINE to LT_TOP_OF_PAGE.
164  ENDENHANCEMENT.
165  *$*$-End:   9999-----------------------------------------------------
166  ENDFORM.
```

⌃ **Figure 3** *Adding Source Code in the Enhancement Block*

6. Click the ENHANCEMENTS button to activate the enhancement, and execute the report to see the result as shown in Figure 4.

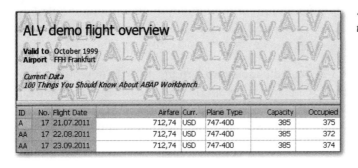

« **Figure 4** *Result of the Enhancement*

Tip 83

Creating Composite Enhancement Implementations to Group Enhancement Implementations Hierarchically

You can create composite enhancement implementations to group enhancement implementations hierarchically for better organization.

When you're creating enhancement implementations, you must assign them to the packages like you do for all other development objects. You can simply group enhancement implementations in packages and package hierarchies to be able to organize them according to categories. However, if you're using enhancement implementations extensively, you might want to look for a better way to organize them. Otherwise, finding the enhancements when you need to modify them in the future will be difficult. You can use composite enhancement implementations to group enhancement implementations hierarchically in a tree structure.

✅ And Here's How ...

Although you don't have to assign composite enhancement implementations to enhancement implementations, it's useful to group enhancement implementations belonging to different packages in composite enhancement implementations. You can even create a single hierarchy for all enhancements on the system. This will give you an alternative way of grouping enhancements, together with using packages and package hierarchies.

To create a composite enhancement implementation, right-click on the package name in the Object Navigator, and use the following menu path on the context menu:

CREATE • ENHANCEMENT • COMPOSITE ENHANCEMENT IMPLEMENTATION

Enter the object name and description as shown in Figure 1, and click the green checkmark button to create the composite enhancement implementation.

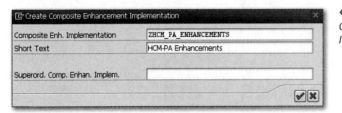

≪ Figure 1 *Creating a Composite Enhancement Implementation*

You can assign a superordinate composite enhancement implementation on the same window to build more detailed hierarchical structure by assigning composite enhancement implementations to each other.

Now, you can assign enhancement implementations to the composite enhancement implementation that you've just created. When creating an enhancement implementation, you can assign it to a composite enhancement implementation directly on the CREATE ENHANCEMENT IMPLEMENTATION window. Select the enhancement from the search help or create a new one using the CREATE button (🗋) as shown in Figure 2.

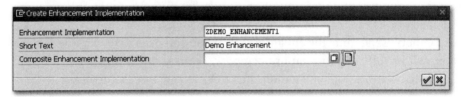

⌃ Figure 2 *Assigning a Composite Enhancement Implementation to an Enhancement Implementation*

In the example shown in Figure 3, a root composite enhancement implementation ZHCM_ENHANCEMENT is created in Package ZENHANCEMENT, and all subordinate composite enhancements and enhancement implementations are linked to this root node.[1]

---

1 Enhancement implementations don't have to be in the same package. Even if they're in different packages, you can see the whole structure in the Object Navigator.

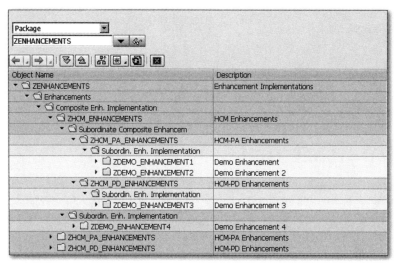

▲ *Figure 3* *Example of a Composite Enhancement Implementation Hierarchy*

Alternatively, you can browse the enhancements in the ENHANCEMENT INFO SYS-TEM. Figure 4 displays the same COMPOSITE ENHANCEMENT IMPLEMENTATION hierarchy in the ENHANCEMENT INFO SYSTEM.

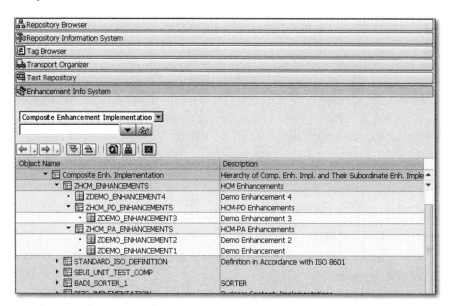

▲ *Figure 4* *Enhancement Info System*

Using Nested Enhancements in Existing Enhancement Implementations[1]

You can nest enhancement implementations to several layers to avoid modifying existing enhancements and losing your enhancement changes later on.

When you create a source code plug-in to implement an implicit or explicit enhancement option, the ENHANCEMENT and ENDENHANCEMENT statements are automatically created, and you can implement custom code between them. Sometimes you may need to modify the existing enhancement implementation. If the enhancement is implemented in the customer namespace, you can simply modify the existing information according to the requirements. However, if the enhancement is an industry-specific implementation, or it's a global implementation running on a country-specific system, it may not be appropriate or even possible to modify the existing enhancement. In this tip, we'll show you how to implement a new enhancement on top of the existing one and separate the different enhancements implemented on the same enhancement point for different purposes.

✓ And Here's How ...

There are implicit enhancement points at the beginning and the end of the enhancement implementations. This helps you nest the enhancements as shown in the example in Figure 1.

---

1 Applicable to SAP NetWeaver release 7.3 and later.

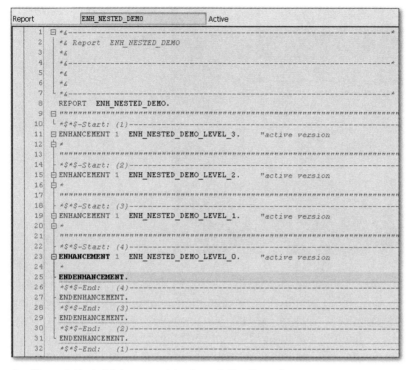

↑ Figure 1 *Nested Enhancement Implementation Example*

Figure 1 shows that Report ENH_NESTED_DEMO is enhanced four times, with each enhancement creating a new level. Let's go over the steps you need to follow to create a nested enhancement using this scenario.

1. Create enhancement implementation ENH_NESTED_DEMO_LEVEL_3.

2. An implicit enhancement point will automatically exist in the enhancement implementation that you created in the previous step. Create a new enhancement implementation ENH_NESTED_DEMO_LEVEL_2.

3. Create as many new levels as you want. In the example in Figure 1, enhancements are nested up to four levels.

Figure 2 illustrates the structure of the enhancement layers created in Figure 1.

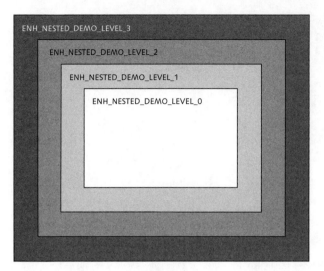

« *Figure 2* *Using Nested Enhancements to Create Enhancement Layers*

Nested enhancements allow you to create enhancement layers as shown in Figure 2. This feature may not be required in small implementations, but if you're using an IS-specific system or a country-specific system implemented by a global company, you're quite likely going to need to enhance the existing enhancements. If you modify the existing enhancement or repair the enhanced code instead of creating nested enhancements, you'll lose the benefits of the Enhancement Framework. If the enhancements are changed in the future, you'll lose all of the modifications that you made on the enhancements. However, if you create a nested enhancement, your enhancements won't be affected by these updates even if the enhancement changes.

Using Enhancements When Modifying Standard ABAP Programs

When you absolutely must modify standard ABAP programs, you can create enhancement points instead of directly modifying the source code when working with the programs.

Suppose you want to implement a customer requirement in an SAP system that forces you to modify the standard ABAP program. When you analyze the implicit and explicit enhancement options in the source code, you find that none of the enhancement options can be used to implement the solution. Although modifying the source code isn't recommended because you'll lose the SAP support on the modified source code and need to perform time-consuming operations on it, you don't have any other option in this case. In this tip, we'll show you a technique that will help you benefit from the Enhancement Framework while modifying the standard ABAP programs.

And Here's How ...

You can normally modify the source code and implement your solution directly in the source code. However, because you always want to use the Enhancement Framework to modify standard SAP programs, you can create an enhancement point at the source code location where you want to modify and implement this custom enhancement point.

Let's walk through an example. Suppose you want to modify Program BCALV_FULLSCREEN_DEMO to add additional logic before the function module call REUSE_ALV_GRID_DISPLAY, and you can't find a suitable enhancement option.

Modify the source code by adding following line just before the function call REUSE_ALV_GRID_DISPLAY:

```
ENHANCEMENT-POINT ZDEMO_ENH SPOTS ZDEMO_SPOT.
```

Here, you can use either an existing enhancement spot or specify a new enhancement spot. When you save the source code, the popup window appears as shown in Figure 1, and the system creates an enhancement spot (if it doesn't exist). After you click the CONTINUE button (✓), the enhancement point will be assigned to the enhancement spot.

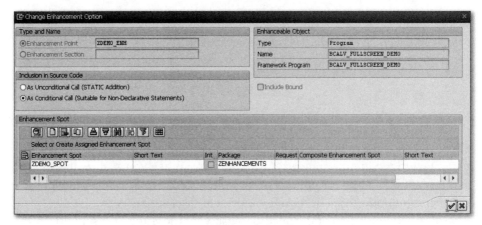

☆ **Figure 1** Assigning an Enhancement Point to the Enhancement Spot

This is the only modification that you must perform; the final appearance of the source code will be as shown in Figure 2.

```
33  *"List Header for Top-Of-Page
34  PERFORM COMMENT_BUILD USING GT_LIST_TOP_OF_PAGE[].
35  (  INSERT        A73K900020                              1
36  ENHANCEMENT-POINT ZDEMO_ENH SPOTS ZDEMO_SPOT .
37  *)  INSERT
38  *"Display List
39  CALL FUNCTION 'REUSE_ALV_GRID_DISPLAY'
40      EXPORTING
41          I_BACKGROUND_ID    = 'ALV_BACKGROUND'
42          i_buffer_active    = 'X'
43          I_CALLBACK_PROGRAM = G_REPID
44          I_STRUCTURE_NAME   = 'SFLIGHT'
```

☆ **Figure 2** Enhancement Point Created in a Standard ABAP Program

You can now make use of all the benefits of the Enhancement Framework. This technique will definitely help you use the Enhancement Framework as a single point of access to all changes on standard objects.

Tip 86

Activating or Deactivating Enhancements with the Switch Framework

You can assign an enhancement implementation's package to a switch to turn the enhancement implementations on and off for different systems.

When you're developing an application that contains enhancement implementations and will be run on different systems, you may need to implement different enhancements according to the configuration on the target system. In this tip, we'll show you how to use the Switch Framework to turn only the required enhancement implementations on and off on the system.

And Here's How ...

All enhancement implementations are switchable by default. However, if you don't assign the package of the enhancement implementation to a switch, it will automatically be active on the system. However, you might want to activate the enhancement only in specific conditions. If you attach a switch to a package of the enhancement, it can be switched on and off on the system using the Switch Framework. You must first create a switch and assign the package of the enhancement implementation to the switch.

Perform the following operations to create a switch and assign the package to it:

1. Go to Transaction SFW1, enter the name of the switch as "ZSWDEMO", and click CREATE.

2. Enter the DESCRIPTION for the switch and click SAVE in the popup dialog that appears.

3. Assign a package and transport request.

4. A switch is created. Navigate to the PACKGS tab and enter the name of the package, whose contents will be made switchable, in the PACKAGES list.

5. Click SAVE (⊞) and then ACTIVATE (⬚) to activate the switch. Activation of the switch runs in the background, so you have to restart the transaction to refresh the object status

You've now created the switch and attached the switch to the package that contains switchable objects. Next, you must assign the switch to a business function. Perform the following steps to create a business function:

1. Go to Transaction SFW2, enter the name of the business function as "ZBFDEMO", and click CREATE.

2. In the popup dialog that appears, enter the DESCRIPTION and LONG TEXT for the business function.

3. Select the TYPE as ENTERPRISE BUSINESS FUNCTION, and click SAVE.

4. Assign a package and transport request.

5. A business function maintenance screen opens. Enter the name of the switch that you created before in the SWITCH list and select TYPE as the ACTIVATION.

6. Navigate to the ATTRIBUTES tab.

7. Check the REVERSIBLE flag to make the business function reversible. This setting allows you to switch off the business function in the future. Otherwise, you can't switch off the business function.

8. Click SAVE (⊞) and ACTIVATE (⬚) to activate the business function. This will also run in the background.

You can check the result of the activation by restarting the transaction. When the business function is activated, you can switch the enhancements on and off in Transaction SFW5. Figure 1 shows the initial view of Transaction SFW5.

Note that business function ZBFDEMO is now on the list. The ⬚ icon indicates that the business function can be reversed, meaning you can activate or deactivate it anytime you want. You can't deactivate the switches that aren't reversible. To activate the switch, select the checkbox on the SCHEDULED STATUS column, and click the ACTIVATE CHANGES button on the toolbar. Activation runs in the background again. When you activate the business function, the icon turns into a yellow bulb (💡).

Name	Description	Scheduled Status
⌂ Check Changes ▮ Activate Changes ❷ Display Legend		
Business Function Set [▼]		
Name	Description	Scheduled Status
▾ ☐		
▾ ☐ ENTERPRISE_BUSINESS_FUNCTIONS	Enterprise Business Functions	
• ⬧ CA_HAP_CI_1	CA, Evaluations, Appraisals, and Surveys 01	☐
• ⬧ CA_PA_CE_GE_QUALI	CA, Employee Qualifications for Concurrent...	☐
• ⬧ DA_ARCHOBJ_STANDARD_1	Data Archiving: Standardization of Archivin...	☐
• ⬧ ILM	Information Lifecycle Management	☐
• ⬧ ILM_RWC_PRODUCT_LIABILITY	Predefined Retention Warehouse Content...	☐
• ⬧ ILM_RWC_TAX	Predefined Retention Warehouse Content...	☐
• ⬧ ILM_RWC_TAX_IS_OIL	Predefined Retention Warehouse Content...	☐
• ⬧ ILM_RWC_TAX_IS_U	ILM: Predef. Ret. Warehouse Content- Ta...	☐
• ⬧ PCA_KEYV	Periodic Key Replacement for Payment Car...	☐
• ⬙ RS_IQM	IQM Reporting (Reversible)	☐
• ⬙ ZBFDEMO	Demonstration of Business Function (Reve...	☐

⌃ **Figure 1** *Changing the Business Function Status*

You can easily switch the enhancement on and off using this technique. When the enhancement is switched off, it's not compiled in the system, which means it won't have any effect on the system performance. You can assign switches to the units that are technically and semantically related and use the business function to maintain the state of the switch.

Tip 87

Adjusting Enhanced Objects When Upgrading the SAP System

When you perform an upgrade to the system or implement a support package, you can access a transaction that will explain which enhancement implementations need to be adjusted.

As we've discussed in other tips, the Enhancement Framework must be the first option to modify or enhance the development object in an SAP system. However, if you perform an upgrade or implement a support package, the enhancements must be adjusted using Transaction SPAU_ENH because the enhanced part of the object might be changed during the upgrade or support package import. In this tip, we'll show you how to use the adjustment tool.

✓ And Here's How ...

When you access Transaction SPAU_ENH after an upgrade or support package implementation, you'll see all of the enhancement implementations that need to be adjusted in a tree as shown in Figure 1.

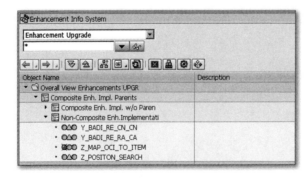

« Figure 1 *Enhancement List in Transaction SPAU_ENH that Need Adjustment*

You must adjust each item in the list individually. The icon beside the enhancement name indicates the adjustment state. Figure 2 shows the possible adjustment statuses that an enhancement can take.

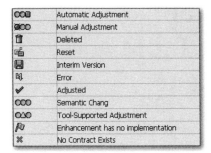

« *Figure 2 Possible Adjustment Statuses*

To start the adjustment, double-click on an enhancement from the list. The ENHANCEMENT IMPLEMENTATION screen opens with an additional ADJUSTMENT tab as shown in Figure 3.

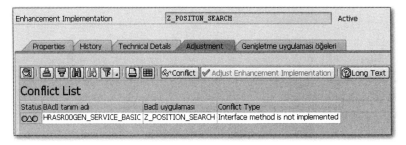

≈ *Figure 3 Adjustment Screen for the Enhancement Implementation*

Double-click on each conflict to see its details. The type of the adjustment will change depending on the enhancement technology used.

Source code conflicts are displayed in the Splitscreen Editor where you can adjust the affected source code. Other types of conflicts are explained with onscreen instructions that you can follow to make the adjustments.

Tip 88

Using the Enhancement Category to Restrict Table and Structure Enhancements

You can restrict the types of enhancements that other people can perform using Customizing includes or append structures to maintain a needed system structure.

The Enhancement Framework allows you to enhance the tables and structures using Customizing includes and append structures. However, structure change can cause many problems within the system. You have to make sure that the change won't affect the objects that depend on the enhanced table or structure. To restrict the types of enhancements that can be implemented on the table or structure, we'll show you how to set up the ENHANCEMENT CATEGORY property for tables and structures.

✓ And Here's How ...

Tables and structures can be enhanced in two ways: Customizing includes and append structures.

Customizing includes are included in the standard structures that are expected to be enhanced with customer-specific fields. The names of the Customizing includes start with "CI_" and are appended in the structure with the `.include` statement, even though they don't exist in the ABAP Data Dictionary. You can create Customizing includes with forward navigation by double-clicking on the name.

Customizing includes are created in the customer namespace. This ensures that the changes won't be overwritten with subsequent upgrades. Figure 1 shows an example table enhanced with three customer-specific fields.

Field	Key	Ini...	Data element	Data T...	Length	Deci...	Short Description
SPCKRIT	☐	☐	QSPCKRIT	CHAR	3	0	SPC Criterion
.INCLUDE	☐	☐	CI_PLMK	STRU	0	0	
ZZMKPREIS	☐	☐	ZZMKPREIS	CURR	11	2	Net price for inspection characteristic
ZZMKEINH	☐	☐	WAERS	CUKY	5	0	Currency Key
ZZCOAREL	☐	☐	ZZCOAREL	CHAR	1	0	CoA relevance

≫ Figure 1 *Enhancing a Standard Table with a Customizing Include*

If Customizing includes aren't available in the structure, the structure still can be enhanced using *append structures*. You can append a structure to the standard tables or structures using the APPEND STRUCTURE button on the toolbar.

A word of warning: be careful when enhancing a structure because it might be included in another structure. The enhanced fields on the structure will immediately be available on the dependent structure. ABAP programs that use the structure can also be affected by the change.

Both options make it pretty easy to enhance the tables and structures. However, the change in the field structure may lead to very serious problems in the system.

Restricting Enhancement Use

If the UNICODE CHECK ACTIVE flag isn't set in the program that uses the structure, the change in the structure may lead to syntax or runtime errors. If the flag is set, the structure change might affect the fragment view of the structure. This change affects the assignments, comparison statements, and accesses with an offset and length. Therefore, you'll need to set the ENHANCEMENT CATEGORY property on the tables and structures to restrict the enhancement on the structures. Set the ENHANCEMENT CATEGORY by choosing EXTRAS • ENHANCEMENT CATEGORY while you're modifying the table or structure definition in Transaction SE11.

You can set the following options for the ENHANCEMENT CATEGORY:

- ► CAN BE ENHANCED (DEEP)
  Enhance the structure with any type of fields.

- ► CAN BE ENHANCED (CHARACTER-TYPE OR NUMERIC)
  Only enhance the structure with character-type or numeric fields.

- ► CAN BE ENHANCED (CHARACTER-TYPE)
  Only enhance the structure with character-type fields.

- ► CANNOT BE ENHANCED
  The structure can't be enhanced.

- ► NOT CLASSIFIED
  The structure isn't classified in any of the enhancement categories.

You must set the ENHANCEMENT CATEGORY for the tables and structures according to these definitions to make sure that the enhancement that will be performed in the future won't affect other development objects that depend on the table or structure.

Creating Multiple-Use Business Add-Ins

You can define a multiple-use Business Add-In that can be implemented many times for different purposes.

Business Add-In (BAdI) technology allows you to define an explicit enhancement point that allows implementers limited access to the original source code. When you implement a BAdI, all of the implementation logic will be in the methods of a custom class that is generated during implementation. You can also define a BAdI that can be implemented multiple times for different purposes; for example, to allow developers to implement different tasks in different conditions after saving data in the application.

✓ And Here's How ...

Before you can create a BAdI definition, you must create an enhancement spot by following these steps:

1. Go to Transaction SE18, enter the name in the ENHANCEMENT SPOT field, and click CREATE.
2. Enter the SHORT TEXT, and click the CREATION OF ENHANCEMENT button (✓).
3. The PACKAGE SELECTION dialog opens. Assign an enhancement spot to a package, and select or create a new transport request.

The enhancement spot is created as shown in Figure 1.

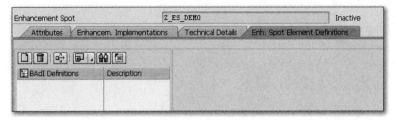

⋩ *Figure 1* *An Empty Enhancement Spot*

Create a BAdI Definition

You can now start creating BAdI definitions in the enhancement spot:

1. Click the CREATE button (⬜) on the toolbar just above the BAdI DEFINITIONS list.

2. Fill in the NAME and SHORT DESCRIPTION fields, and click the CONTINUE button (✅). An empty BAdI definition will be created as shown in Figure 2.

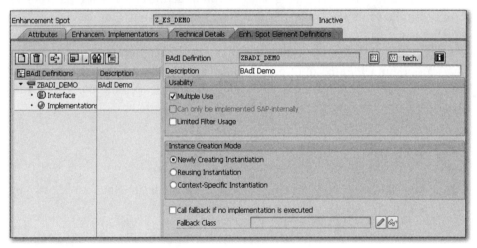

⋩ *Figure 2* *An Empty BAdI Definition*

3. To enable multiple implementations for the BAdI, make sure that the MULTIPLE USE checkbox in the USABILITY section is checked.

Define an Interface

Now you need to define the interface that will be used to interact between the BAdI and the original source code:

1. Open the tree in the BADI DEFINITIONS list, and double-click on the INTERFACE icon.

2. Enter the name in the INTERFACE field, and click the CHANGE INTERFACE button (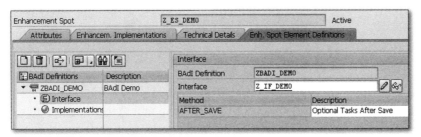).

3. Confirm the popup that asks you if you want to create the interface.

4. Assign a package, and select a transport request.

5. Create a method in the interface, and define method parameters.

6. Save and activate both the interface and enhancement spot. The result will be as shown in Figure 3.

⌃ **Figure 3** *Business Add-In Example*

Now your BAdI is ready to use and can be implemented several times.

Note that you can't use the EXPORTING or RETURNING parameters for multiple-use BAdIs. It would be meaningless to return the same variable from multiple implementations. However, you can use the CHANGING parameter in multiple-use BAdIs. If you change the parameter in one implementation, the changed value will be used in the next implementation.

Tip 90

Using Filters to Select Between Multiple BAdI Implementations

You can define a filter for a BAdI to allow developers to implement the same BAdI several times each for different filter values.

When you're developing an application that will run on several systems, defining BAdIs helps other developers easily adapt your application into their organizations. There might also be cases in which different logics must be implemented in the same BAdI, and the implementations must be filtered according to the runtime values.

Normally, you can define a BAdI and provide the critical variables as an interface parameter, and the developer can implement the whole logic in the same implementation using `IF` or `CASE` statements. Alternatively, you can define a filter for a BAdI to allow developers to create multiple BAdI implementations and run them according to the filter values.

✔ And Here's How ...

You can create a filter for a BAdI in the enhancement spot where the BAdI is created. To do this, follow these steps:

1. Go to Transaction SE18 and open the enhancement spot in change mode. You can use the CREATE BADI SUBOBJECT button to create a filter as shown in Figure 1.

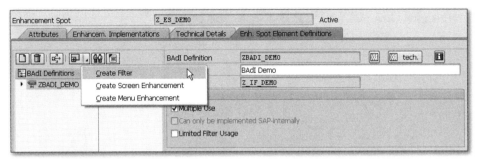

⋟ *Figure 1* *Creating a Filter—Step 1*

2. In the popup that appears, enter the filter details as shown in Figure 2.

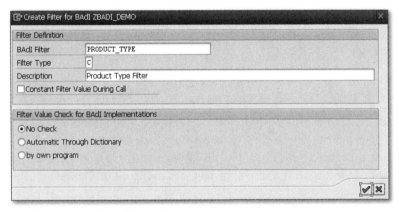

⋟ *Figure 2* *Creating a Filter—Step 2*

3. Click the CONTINUE button (✔) to finish the operation.

Now you can assign different product types for different implementations. Perform the following operations to assign a filter to the implementation:

1. Open the enhancement implementation in Transaction SE19.

2. Open the tree for the relevant implementation in the BADI IMPLEMENTATIONS list, and double-click on the FILTER VAL. item.

3. Click on the CREATE FILTER COMBINATION button (□ Combination).

4. An empty filter combination is created. Select the created row, and click the CHANGE FILTER VALUE button (✎ Filt. Val.)

5. Enter the filter details as shown in Figure 3.

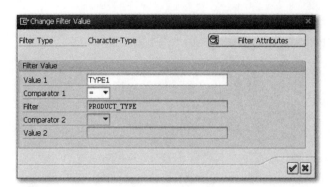

《 Figure 3 *Assigning a Filter to an Implementation*

6. Click the CONTINUE button (✓) to finish the assignment. Save and activate the enhancement implementation.

You can now use the filter in the ABAP program where the BAdI is called using the following syntax:

```
GET BADI handle FILTERS product_type = product_type.
call badi handle->calculate_tax.
```

As you see in the example, you can call enhancement implementations dynamically depending on the runtime values. This is quite useful if you can guess the parameter that can be used as a filter. On the other hand, it's also practical to implement BAdIs according to the filters, instead of coding all of the logic in the ABAP program.

Finding BAdIs in SAP Transactions Using the ABAP Debugger

You can use debugging techniques to find BAdIs that are available in a transaction.

There are two types of Business Add-Ins defined in the SAP system: classic BAdIs and new BAdIs. Classic BAdIs were introduced with release 4.6; since SAP NetWeaver 7.0 has been released, BAdIs have been redesigned to be an important part of the Enhancement Framework. All BAdIs are explicitly defined by SAP in standard transactions to help developers adapt these transactions to specific requirements.

Sometimes, it might be difficult to find the existing BAdIs in an SAP transaction. You can use the ABAP Debugger tool to find the BAdIs—both classic and new—that are defined in a standard transaction.

And Here's How ...

BAdIs are called in ABAP programs in two ways depending on the type of the BAdI. We'll discuss how to find each type of BAdI in the following sections.

Finding Classic BAdIs

Classic BAdIs are instantiated with the GET_INSTANCE static method of the CL_ EXITHANDLER class. If you put a breakpoint into the method and call a transaction, the execution will stop every time the program tries to instantiate a BAdI.

Let's put a breakpoint in the method and call Transaction VA01 as an example. Figure 1 shows the ABAP Debugger screen that is displayed when the ABAP program tries to instantiate a classic BAdI.

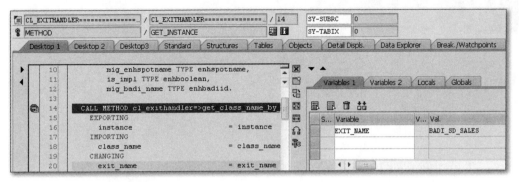

⋩ *Figure 1 A Classic BAdI Call Caught in the ABAP Debugger*

As you can see, when you enter Transaction VA01 the program tries to instantiate BADI_SD_SALES. You can now use Transaction SE18 to see the definition of the BAdI and check whether it can be used. If not, you can execute the debugger by pressing F8 to see if there are more BAdIs.

Finding New BAdIs

New BAdIs are instantiated using the ABAP statement GET BADI. This time, you can create a breakpoint to stop at the GET BADI command to see if a new BAdI is available in the same transaction.

Switch on debugging using the /h command, and enter Transaction VA01 again. In the ABAP Debugger, select the following menu path to set the breakpoint:

> BREAKPOINTS • BREAKPOINT AT • BREAKPOINT AT STATEMENT

Enter the statement "GET_BADI" on the popup. Now, execute the debugger by pressing F8 to see if there are any BAdI calls in the transaction. Figure 2 shows the ABAP Debugger screen when the execution reaches the GET BADI statement.

This time the BAdI type can be seen on the declaration statement of the l_badi variable, which is again BADI_SD_SALES.

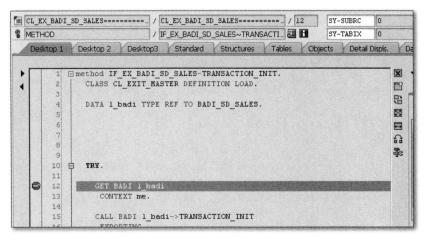

⌃ *Figure 2 New BAdI Call Caught in the ABAP Debugger*

Although you can find the list of available BAdIs in the SAP documentation (and you should read the documentation before implementing it), sometimes using these techniques saves you from having to find the BAdI in the documentation.

Tip 92

Creating Customized Transactions with Transaction Variants

You can tailor and customize transactions to suit your business needs by modifying different aspects of transactions with transaction variants.

In some cases, you might want to customize a business transaction by modifying the field attributes on the screen. This customization can be either hiding a screen field or inserting a default value into a screen field and making it read-only. We'll show you how to achieve this using transaction variants, which allows you to create a tailored version of a standard transaction by modifying attributes of the screen fields.

✓ And Here's How ...

Suppose you want to modify the initial screen of Transaction MM01 (used to create materials). Figure 1 shows the initial screen that you're going to customize.

« *Figure 1* *Transaction MM01 Initial Screen*

Suppose, for example, you want to perform the following adjustments on the screen:

▸ Hide the Copy from... Material field.

▸ Disable the Change Number field.

▸ Insert the Raw Material for Material Type field and make it read-only.

▸ Insert the Chemical Industry for Industry Sector but leave it modifiable.

To accomplish this, follow these steps to create the transaction variant:

1. Go to Transaction SHD0, and enter "MM01" in the Transaction Code field.

2. Click Create (□) on the toolbar.

3. Click Continue (✔) on the information popup to proceed.

4. Select Industry Sector as Chemical Industry, and select Material Type as Raw Material.

5. Press ⌨Enter to proceed. A confirmation dialog opens on which you can see the filled values and adjust the screen modifications as shown in Figure 2.

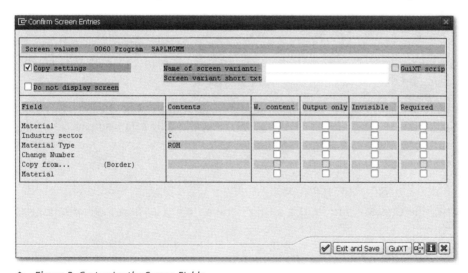

⌃ **Figure 2** *Customize the Screen Fields*

All screen elements are listed on the screen. Select the following appropriate options (if logically possible) for each field:

▸ W. Content
Saves the value you entered as the default value for the screen field.

▶ OUTPUT ONLY
Makes the screen field read-only.

▶ INVISIBLE
Hides the field from the screen.

▶ REQUIRED
Makes the screen field required.

6. Enter the name and description for the screen variant, and select the fields as shown in Figure 3 to adjust the screen according to your requirements.

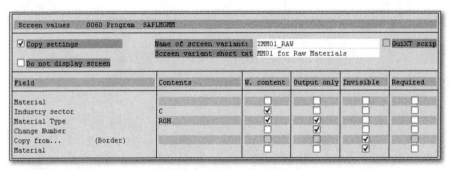

≫ **Figure 3** *Customize the Screen Fields*

7. Click EXIT and SAVE to finish the operation. The screen variant details are displayed on the screen. Save and exit the screen.

You're now in the TRANSACTION VARIANT maintenance screen. Make sure you're in the TRANSACTION VARIANTS tab, and perform the following steps to create the transaction variant and assign the screen variant that you created in the previous steps:

1. Enter the name of the transaction variant.

2. Click the CHANGE button (🖊) on the toolbar in the ASSIGN SCREEN VARIANTS section.

3. Click the INSERT ROW button (📲).

4. Enter the name of the screen variant that you created in the previous steps (see Figure 3).

5. Click the SAVE ASSIGNMENT button (💾).

6. Select GOTO • CREATE VARIANT TRANSACTION from the menu. The Create Transaction dialog opens. Enter "ZMM01_RAW" in the TRANSACTION CODE field.

7. Enter a description in the SHORT TEXT field, and click the CONTINUE button (☑).

8. The CREATE VARIANT TRANSACTION screen opens. Save and exit to finish the process.

The transaction variant is ready to use now. You can test it using Transaction ZMM01_RAW. The result should be as shown in Figure 4.

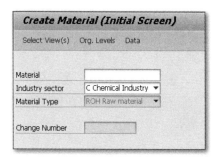

« Figure 4 *Transaction MM01 with Customized Screen Fields*

As you see in Figure 4, the screen fields are customized according to the custom requirements. You can create different variants for the same transaction for different user groups. It's very practical to perform these kinds of basic changes on the screen without making any modifications.

Tip 93

Using Parameter Transactions to Create a Transaction for Table Maintenance Dialogs

To allow users to maintain database table entries, you can assign a transaction code to a table maintenance dialog of a database table by creating a parameter transaction.

Table maintenance dialogs are very helpful for maintaining and transporting entries for database tables. They are also fairly easy for end users to use. You can access the table maintenance dialog of a table using Transaction SM30. Normally, if you want to restrict the user access for table maintenance, you can set the authorization group property and assign users to this authorization group. Alternatively, and probably more practically, you can create parameter transactions to assign a transaction code for the maintenance screen of a single database table, and end users can use this transaction code to access the maintenance screen of a table.

✓ And Here's How ...

Parameter transactions are created in Transaction SE93 as for other types of transactions. Perform the following steps to create a parameter transaction:

1. Go to Transaction SE93, enter the transaction code, and click CREATE.

2. On the popup dialog, fill in the SHORT TEXT field, and select START OBJECT as TRANSACTION WITH PARAMETERS.

3. Click the CONTINUE button (✓). When the CREATE PARAMETER screen opens, enter "SM30" in the TRANSACTION field.

4. Select the SKIP INITIAL SCREEN checkbox.

5. Click checkbox INSERT ROW button (⊞) on the DEFAULT VALUES table control to insert the default values for the screen fields. Fill in the table as shown in Figure 1.

« **Figure 1** *Default Values for Transaction SM30*

6. Enter the name of the table that you want to maintain as a value for the VIEW-NAME field. You must also enter "X" as a value for the UPDATE field. If you want to perform another action, you must set one of the following fields to X:

 ▸ UPDATE: Maintain

 ▸ SHOW: Display

 ▸ TRANSPORT: Transport

 ▸ UPDATE_LTD: Maintain subset

 ▸ SHOW_LTD: Display subset

 ▸ TRANSP_LTD: Transport subset

7. Save and exit to finish the process.

Now when you go to the transaction code, it will take you directly to the maintenance screen as if you entered Transaction SM30, entered the table name in the TABLE/VIEW field, and clicked the MAINTAIN button. You can use the same technique for any generic transaction to create transaction codes for special requirements.

Tip 94

Using SET/GET Parameters to Assign Default Values for Screen Elements

You can use the SET/GET parameters to assign default values to certain screen elements and make the lives of end users much easier!

When you're developing an ABAP program, it's very important to give end users the best possible experience when using the program screens. For example, if there's a screen field that the end user needs to enter in many screens, but the value of this field is constant most of the time (not always), the end user doesn't want to fill this field in every time. You can use SET/GET parameters to assign default values so that end users don't have to repeatedly type in the same value.

✓ And Here's How ...

You can assign a default value on the user's master record at the user level. Whenever a screen field with this parameter appears on the screen, the field value is automatically populated. Even if the parameter isn't defined on the user's master record, the parameter value is stored to the memory after the user enters a value to the screen field the first time.

Note that you should only use the SET/GET parameters for fields that don't change frequently during the user session. If you use the SET/GET parameters for screen fields that usually take different values, it can even be frustrating for the end user to change the value every time.

The value of the SET/GET parameters can also be updated with ABAP commands during the current user session, but all of the changes are cleared when the user logs off. Let's see the details to understand how SET/GET parameters are used in the system.

Create the SET/GET Parameter

First, you must create the SET/GET parameters to be able to assign them to the users. Perform the following operations to create SET/GET parameters:

1. Go to Transaction SE80 to open the Object Navigator.

2. Select WORKBENCH • EDIT OBJECT, and navigate to the MORE tab.

3. Enter "ZTEST" in the SET/GET PARAMETER ID field, and select the radio button beside this field.

4. Click the CREATE button (🗔) to finish.

Assign the Parameter in the User Master Record

You can now assign the parameter in the user's master record by following these steps:

1. Go to Transaction SU01, and open the user maintenance screen for the end user that you want to assign the SET/GET parameters to.

2. Navigate to the PARAMETERS tab, and fill in the parameter as shown in Figure 1.

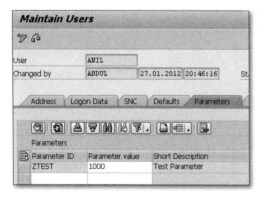

《 Figure 1 Assigning a Parameter Value in the User Master Record

The parameter is ready, and it can be used in the selection screen and dialog screens. If you want to use it on the selection screens, you should use the following syntax:

```
PARAMETERS: p_test(4) TYPE n MEMORY ID ztest.
```

When you run the program for the first time, it's filled with the value you defined in the user's master record. If you change to a different value, the next time, the field is populated with the new value until the user logs off the system.

You can also assign the parameter to the fields on the dialog screens as shown in Figure 2.

《 Figure 2 *Assigning SET/GET Parameters to the Screen Field*

If you select the checkbox GET PARAMETER, the screen field is populated from memory using the parameter ID entered in the PARAMETER ID field.

If you select the checkbox SET PARAMETER, the parameter value is updated in the memory when the user changes the value on the screen.

You can also read and update the parameter value in the ABAP programs using the following syntax:

```
GET PARAMETER ID 'ZTEST' FIELD lv_get.
SET PARAMETER ID 'ZTEST' FIELD lv_set.
```

On the first line, the parameter value is transferred to the variable lv_get. Then, the parameter value in the memory is updated with the value of the lv_set variable on the second line.

Assign SET/GET Parameters to Data Elements

You can also assign SET/GET parameters to the data elements as shown in Figure 3.

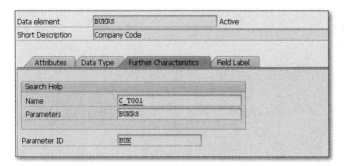

« *Figure 3 Assigning
SET/GET Parameter BUK to
the Data Element BUKRS*

Here, the parameter BUK is assigned to the data element BUKRS. Whenever a
screen field with data element BUKRS is created, the SET/GET parameter BUK is
automatically assigned to this field.

Part 9

Web Dynpro ABAP

Things You'll Learn in this Section

Web Dynpro ABAP is SAP's strategic UI technology that can be used to create web interfaces. It allows you to separate the presentation layer from the business logic and develop web applications without knowing any web programming languages. The tools to develop Web Dynpro ABAP components are fully integrated in the ABAP Workbench. This part provides tips and tricks to help you use specific configuration options for Web Dynpro applications. You'll also learn how to use the specific ABAP Workbench tools, such as the debugger for Web Dynpro ABAP applications.

Tip **95**

Controlling the Runtime Behavior of Web Dynpro ABAP Applications with Application Parameters

If you have custom requirements, you can use application parameters to control the runtime behavior of Web Dynpro ABAP applications.

When you're developing a Web Dynpro ABAP application, you might need to change the runtime behavior of the application to meet any custom requirements. Several predefined application parameters can be configured at the application level or globally on the system to meet these requirements, which can't be achieved most of the time by changing the source code.

✓ And Here's How ...

You can maintain application parameters in two ways.

Change Attribute for One Application

If you want to change the attribute for a single specific Web Dynpro ABAP application, you can maintain the values in the PARAMETERS tab of the Web Dynpro ABAP application maintenance screen. Perform the following steps to maintain the application parameters:

1. Open the Web Dynpro ABAP application in the ABAP Workbench.

2. Open the application maintenance screen by double-clicking on the application name on the object tree.

3. Navigate to the PARAMETERS tab.

4. Select the PARAMETER using the search help, and maintain its value in the VALUE field.

You can select from several types of predefined parameters offered by the Web Dynpro ABAP framework as shown in Figure 1. For example, you can use the parameter WDDISABLEUSERPERSONALIZATION to switch off the personalization feature for the end users. It's also possible to add a custom parameter and use it in the Web Dynpro ABAP application.

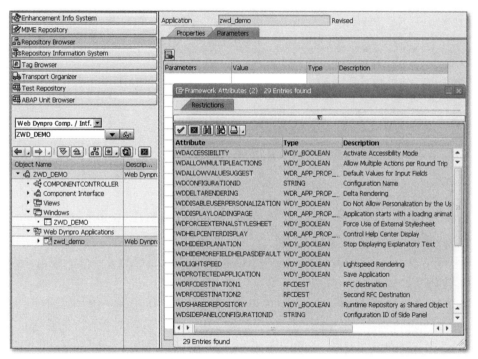

≫ **Figure 1** *Maintaining Application Parameters for a Web Dynpro ABAP Application*

Change Attribute for All Applications

You can use the application parameters when you create more than one application for the same component, and you want to change the behavior of the same component for each Web Dynpro application. If you want to configure the parameters globally for all applications, the Web Dynpro application *wd_global_setting* can be used with the following URL:

http://<server>:<port>/sap/bc/webdynpro/sap/wd_global_setting

A configuration screen opens as shown in Figure 2.

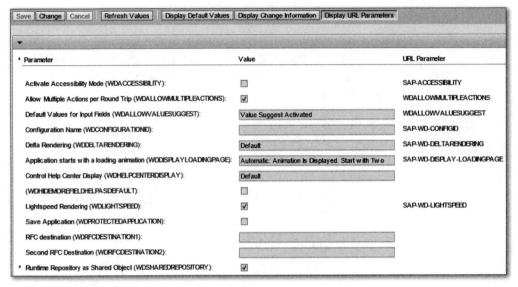

⋩ *Figure 2 Changing Application Parameters Globally*

The change you make on this screen will be valid for all Web Dynpro applications. Using this screen, you can change the following options:

▸ General system parameters such as enabling accessibility, delta rendering options, or display options for loading animation

▸ Adjustment parameters such as enabling or disabling the personalization globally

▸ Design parameters such as toolbar design, label alignment, or stylesheet options

▸ Side panel parameters to configure the side panel

If you set a different value at the application level for specific Web Dynpro applications, the value at the application level will override the value coming from the global configuration.

Tip 96

Tailoring Web Dynpro ABAP Applications to User Groups with Application and Component Configuration

You can create component and application configurations to modify the behavior of the Web Dynpro applications for different target groups.

When you develop a Web Dynpro ABAP application, sometimes you need to design the application so it can meet the requirements of different user groups. In this tip, we'll show you how to meet these requirements by creating multiple sets of application and component configurations for Web Dynpro applications. This will allow you to make small changes to the attributes of the screen elements for each configuration and assign them to the different user groups according to their requirements. You can also publish the same application to the different user groups only with small changes.

✓ And Here's How ...

To create a new configuration, first create different component configurations, and modify the behavior of the application in the configurations. Then you can create application configurations for each component configuration and assign these application configurations to the Web Dynpro ABAP applications. For example, you can hide screen elements using the application and component configurations.

Let's walk through the different steps—you first create a component configuration by doing the following:

1. Go to Transaction SE80 and open the Web Dynpro component that you want to configure.

2. On the object tree, right-click on the component name and select the CREATE/ CHANGE CONFIGURATION option from the context menu.

3. The configuration editor opens in a browser window as shown in Figure 1.

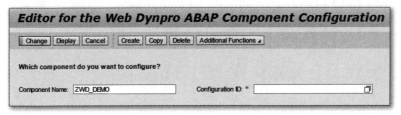

⌃ *Figure 1 Configuration Editor for Component Configuration*

4. Enter the name of the CONFIGURATION ID in the field and click the CREATE button.

5. Enter the DESCRIPTION and PACKAGE name and click OK.

6. Assign a TRANSPORT REQUEST and click OK.

7. A configuration window opens. Expand the view name on the left table, and the screen elements will be displayed as shown in Figure 2.

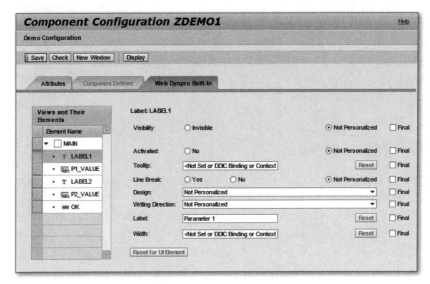

⌃ *Figure 2 Component Configuration*

8. Select the screen element that you want to hide from the tree. Attributes that can be configured using the configuration settings are displayed on the right side.

9. Set the VISIBILITY property as INVISIBLE.

10. Save and close the browser window.

You can see the created component configuration on the object tree by clicking the REFRESH button as shown in Figure 3.

⨠ *Figure 3 Displaying the Component Configuration in an Object Tree*

Your second main step is to create an application configuration and assign the component configuration to the application configuration. Perform the following steps:

1. Go to Transaction SE80 and open the Web Dynpro component.

2. On the object tree, right-click on the Web Dynpro application, and select the CREATE/CHANGE CONFIGURATION option from the context menu. The configuration editor opens in a browser window.

3. Enter the name of the CONFIGURATION ID and click the CREATE button.

4. Enter the DESCRIPTION and PACKAGE name and click OK.

5. Assign a TRANSPORT REQUEST and click OK.

6. The APPLICATION CONFIGURATION screen opens; assign the component configuration that you created in the previous step. The result should be as shown as in Figure 4.

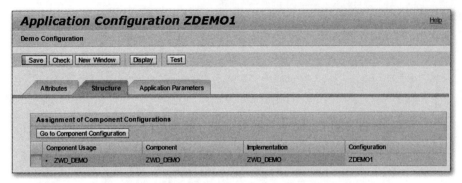

≫ *Figure 4 Application Configuration*

7. Save the configuration and close the browser. You can see the created application configuration on the object tree by clicking the REFRESH button as shown in Figure 5.

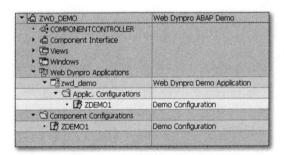

≪ *Figure 5 Displaying the Application Configuration in an Object Tree*

8. You can now run the application with the configured settings by right-clicking on the application configuration and selecting TEST from the context menu.

Customizing Logon Screens for Web Dynpro ABAP Applications

You can customize the logon screens for Web Dynpro ABAP applications to meet different custom requirements for end users and improve usability and security.

If you run the Web Dynpro ABAP application directly without portal integration, the standard logon screen is displayed with default elements, which may not be suitable for end users. We'll show you how to use the system logon configuration options to define which fields are displayed on the screen and how to change the screen layout to meet different custom requirements.

✓ And Here's How ...

When you run the Web Dynpro ABAP application directly without portal integration, the standard logon screen will be displayed as shown in Figure 1.

This screen may not be suitable for end users, especially if you're publishing the application to users who don't have much technical background. No elements should be on the screen that the end user doesn't need to see or modify.

You can customize this screen by changing the system logon configuration options on the related node in Transaction SICF. Perform the following steps to change the logon screen for a Web Dynpro ABAP application:

⌃ **Figure 1** *Standard Logon Screen for Web Dynpro Applications*

1. Go to Transaction SICF, and find the node for the Web Dynpro ABAP application for which you want to create a custom logon screen. You can find your node easily by entering the Web Dynpro ABAP application name in the SERVICE NAME field and executing the screen (see Figure 2).

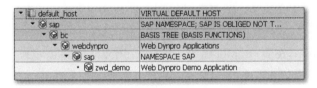

≪ Figure 2 *Web Dynpro ABAP Application in Transaction SICF*

2. Double-click on the application node to navigate to the CREATE/CHANGE A SERVICE screen.

3. Navigate to the ERROR PAGES tab.

4. Select the SYSTEM LOGON radio button in the LOGON ERRORS tab.

5. Click on the CONFIGURATION button beside the SYSTEM LOGON radio button to open the SYSTEM LOGON CONFIGURATION dialog.

6. Select the DEFINE SERVICE SPECIFIC SETTINGS radio button, and all of the customizable elements are activated as shown in Figure 3.

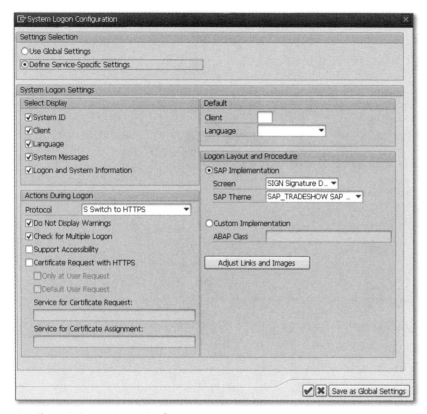

⌃ *Figure 3* System Logon Configuration Options

You can perform the following configurations on the logon screen using the SYSTEM LOGON CONFIGURATION dialog:

▶ Select the fields that should be displayed on the logon screen.

▶ Change the actions that should be performed in different situations during logon.

▶ Set default values for the CLIENT and LANGUAGE fields.

▶ Change the layout of the logon screen by selecting the screen and theme.

▶ Create a new class by inheriting the CL_ICF_SYSTEM_LOGIN class to create your own login page.

▶ Adjust the links and images on the logon screen.

Perform the following changes to create a customized logon screen:

1. Hide the System ID and Language fields, and put a default value in the Client field.

2. Select NetWeaver from the Screen combo box in the Logon Layout and Procedure section.

The result will be as shown in Figure 4.

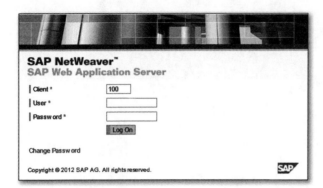

≪ *Figure 4 Customized Logon Screen*

You now have a suitable screen to publish your application to external users such as customers or partners.

Enhancing Web Dynpro ABAP Applications in the Enhancement Framework

You don't have to modify the original object to enhance Web Dynpro ABAP applications to meet custom requirements—instead, you can use different enhancement techniques in the Enhancement Framework.

Web Dynpro ABAP became the standard UI technology for developing web applications in the ABAP Workbench after the advancement in web technologies. These Web Dynpro ABAP components need to be modified like other ABAP programs to fit custom requirements. In this tip, we'll show you the specific techniques offered by the Enhancement Framework to enhance Web Dynpro ABAP components, which will save you a lot of time and effort during system upgrades.

✅ And Here's How ...

SAP has introduced the following Web Dynpro ABAP special enhancement techniques to enhance Web Dynpro ABAP components:

- Create or delete UI elements
- Create context nodes and attributes
- Create a new view to the component
- Add a view or navigation link to the existing window
- Create a method or add pre/post/overwrite exits
- Create a new attribute, event, or action

► Create a new inbound and outbound plug

► Add component or controller usage

Let's see how Web Dynpro ABAP applications can be enhanced using the demo application WDT_TABLE. Figure 1 shows the initial view of the application.

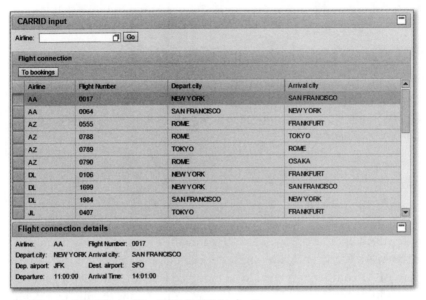

⌃ *Figure 1 Initial View of the WDT_TABLE Application*

In the initial screen, you can select any row to see the flight connection details from the table. Suppose you want to see the departure and arrival times on the table. This information already exists but can only be seen on the details part, so it's easy to add this attribute into the table with the following enhancement steps:

1. Go to Transaction SE80 and open the Web Dynpro ABAP component WDT_TABLE.

2. Open View VIEW_1, and navigate to the LAYOUT tab.

3. Click the ENHANCE button (⊚) on the toolbar.

4. Enter the NAME and DESCRIPTION of the enhancement implementation in the popup dialog.

5. Add the departure and arrival time columns into the table and bind them with the DEPTIME and ARRTIME attributes in the SPFLI_NODE context node.

6. Save and activate the changes.

You can now run the application and see that the departure and arrival time information has been added into the table as shown in Figure 2.

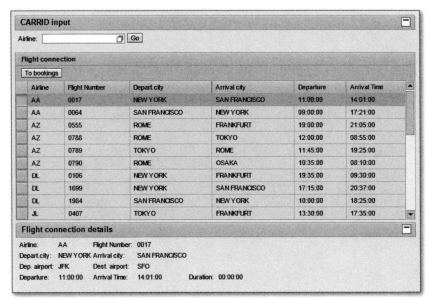

⌃ **Figure 2** *Enhanced View of the WDT_TABLE Application*

As shown in the example, Web Dynpro ABAP is tightly integrated with the Enhancement Framework, which makes it easy to adopt Web Dynpro ABAP applications into your system without modifying the original object.

Tip 99

Debugging Web Dynpro-Specific Program Entities

You can use the Web Dynpro tool in the ABAP Debugger to debug and analyze Web Dynpro ABAP applications.

Web Dynpro ABAP applications can be debugged by setting external breakpoints in the source code at relevant positions. This technique is used not only for Web Dynpro ABAP applications, but also for all types of programs that run outside the SAP GUI. The ABAP Debugger has an additional tool called the *Web Dynpro tool* that's designed to help developers debug Web Dynpro applications. In this tip, we'll show you how to use the Web Dynpro tool to debug Web Dynpro-specific program entities.

✔ And Here's How ...

Debugging a Web Dynpro ABAP application is as easy as debugging a normal ABAP program. You only need to set an external breakpoint into the source code to start the Web Dynpro application in debug mode. You can set external breakpoints using the SET/DELETE EXTERNAL BREAKPOINT button (⬛) on the toolbar while the cursor is in the position where you want to start the debugger. When the program execution reaches the external breakpoint, it stops, and the ABAP Debugger session is started in a new SAP GUI session.

Now you can start using the Web Dynpro tool. Add the Web Dynpro tool into the Debugger Desktop using the NEW TOOL button (⬛) on the right part of any tool on the desktop. Select the Web Dynpro tool in the SPECIAL TOOLS folder, and the Web Dynpro tool is added into the existing desktop. Figure 1 shows an example view of the Web Dynpro tool.

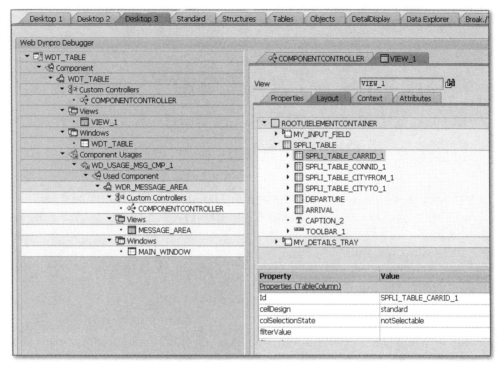

⋩ *Figure 1* Web Dynpro Tool in the ABAP Debugger

The tool has so many features that it can't be used efficiently in a small window as a part of the Debugger Desktop. As shown in Figure 1, you can close all of the other tools on the desktop to use the Web Dynpro tool more efficiently.

You can see all entities of the Web Dynpro component in a hierarchy and see the details of the entity by double-clicking it. For example, double-click on the view name to open the detailed view to see layout elements, context entities, and attributes.

If you want to navigate to the runtime object, you can right-click on the entity on the left tree and select DISPLAY RUNTIME OBJECT. You can also navigate to the definition of the object in the ABAP Workbench using the DISPLAY WORKBENCH OBJECT option in the same context menu.

Web Dynpro ABAP applications are much different from normal ABAP programs in both design and runtime perspectives. That's why you need a special tool to debug and analyze these applications. Otherwise, it would be very difficult to analyze the Web Dynpro ABAP applications using the standard ABAP Debugger tools.

Assigning a Transaction Code to a Web Dynpro Application Using a Parameter Transaction

You can assign a transaction code for Web Dynpro ABAP applications so end users can start the application directly in the SAP GUI without needing to provide a username or password.

You may sometimes need to assign Web Dynpro applications to users who usually use the SAP GUI for their daily work. However, when you or a user is accessing a Web Dynpro ABAP application directly from the browser, you'll usually need to provide a username and password or configure a single sign-on (SSO). Sometimes, you may need to allow the user to access the applications from the SAP GUI without providing a username or password. To solve this problem, you can create a transaction code for the Web Dynpro ABAP application that allows end users to start the application either in the SAP GUI or the web browser using the transaction code without having to provide a username or password.

✓ And Here's How ...

Parameter transactions allow you to assign specific values to the fields on a transaction's initial screen, so you can skip the initial screen. This allows you to create several transaction codes for the same transaction for different purposes. This is very useful when your end users frequently use the SAP GUI, and you don't want them to start any other application to run the Web Dynpro ABAP application.

You can use Transaction WDYID to create a transaction code for the Web Dynpro ABAP applications using the parameter transaction technique. Let's create a transaction code for Web Dynpro ABAP application WDT_TABLE. Perform the following steps to create the transaction:

1. Go to Transaction SE93.

2. Enter "ZWD_TEST" in the TRANSACTION CODE field and click CREATE.

3. Enter a short text, and select TRANSACTION WITH PARAMETERS in the START OBJECT section.

4. Enter "WDYID" in the TRANSACTION field, and select the SKIP INITIAL SCREEN checkbox.

5. In the DEFAULT VALUES table, enter "WDT_TABLE" for the APPLICATION field and enter "Browser" for the STARTMODE field. The result will be as shown as in Figure 1.

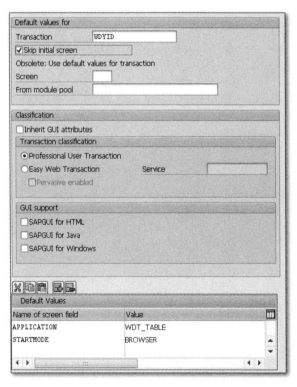

« *Figure 1* *Creating a Parameter Transaction for a Web Dynpro Application*

When you run the transaction in the SAP GUI, the Web Dynpro application starts in a new browser window. You now don't need to provide a username and password. Authentication is performed using an SSO mechanism. If you change the

STARTMODE field value to the GUI instead of BROWSER, the application starts within the SAP GUI window as shown in Figure 2.

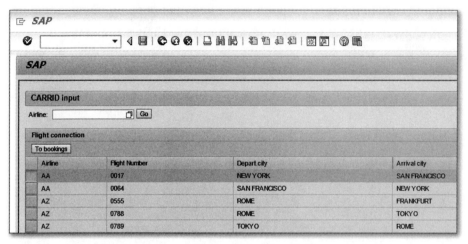

⌃ *Figure 2 Starting a Web Dynpro Application within the SAP GUI*

Users can run the transaction just like they would when running other transactions; they may not even realize that they are using a Web Dynpro ABAP application instead of the normal SAP GUI application.

The Author

Abdulbasıt Gülşen is a senior SAP technology consultant focusing on both the ABAP and Java application environments of SAP. He started his career working as a software developer for an SAP customer. He moved to an SAP partner to work as a consultant after 2 years and has continued working as a technology consultant for 10 years.

He has ABAP development experience on several platforms (SAP ECC, SAP CRM, HR, IS-U) and in diverse industries, as well as experience in other SAP platforms and tools, such as SAP NetWeaver BPM, Portal, and Web Dynpro ABAP/Java. He's been certified in the ABAP Workbench, SAP NetWeaver Portal development, and SAP NetWeaver Portal administration.

Abdulbasıt is also an active contributor on the SAP Community Network (SCN) and organizes local SAP community events in Turkey. In early 2012, he was selected as an SAP Mentor based on his contributions to the SAP community.

Index

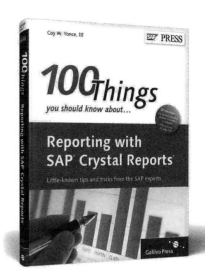

- Provides 100 little-known time-saving tips and workarounds for SAP Crystal Reports users

- Learn quickly with hands-on instructions and many screenshots

- Gives you the tools for increasing efficiency and getting the most out of SAP Crystal Reports

Coy W. Yonce, III

100 Things You Should Know About Reporting with SAP Crystal Reports

Have you ever spent hours on a report only to discover that you could have saved time with a simple tip? If so, you'll be delighted with this book, which unlocks the secrets of reporting with SAP Crystal Reports. Its 100 tips and workarounds will help you increase productivity, save time, and improve the overall ease-of-use of SAP Crystal Reports. With this book, you will accomplish your reporting needs faster, more easily, and more effectively.

338 pp., 2012, 49,95 Euro / US$ 49.95
ISBN 978-1-59229-390-2

www.sap-press.com

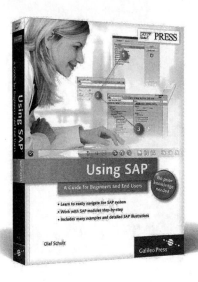

■ Learn to easily navigate
the SAP system

■ Work with SAP modules
step-by-step

■ Includes many examples and
detailed SAP illustrations

Olaf Schulz

Using SAP:
A Guide for Beginners and End Users

This book helps end users and beginners get started in SAP ERP and
provides readers with the basic knowledge they need for their daily
work. Readers will get to know the essentials of working with the SAP
system, learn about the SAP systems' structures and functions, and
discover how SAP connects to critical business processes. Whether
this book is used as an exercise book or as a reference book, readers
will find what they need to help them become more comfortable
with SAP ERP.

388 pp., 2012, 39,95 Euro / US$ 39.95
ISBN 978-1-59229-408-4

www.sap-press.com